THE
FAILURE
OF THE
STATE

Essays on the Democratic Costs of Government

by

Rodney Atkinson

Published by
Compuprint Publishing
4 Sands Road
Swalwell Industrial Estate
Tyne and Wear NE16 3DJ
Tel: 091 488 8936

Copyright © Compuprint Publishing 1989

ISBN 0 9509353 3 6

Price: £5.95

Typesetting by Auckland VidiSet Ltd
7 Barge Court, Waterside
44-48 Wharf Road, London N1 7SH
Tel: 01-490 2929   Fax: 01-250 0044

Printed and Bound in Great Britain at
The Camelot Press Ltd, Southampton

Contents

The Author

Rodney Atkinson was born in Gosforth Northumberland in 1948. He has a BA Honours degree from Newcastle University and an MSc from Durham University. He lectured at the University of Mainz, West Germany before returning to take up senior managerial posts in merchant banking in the City of London. He now runs his own businesses while writing books, articles and papers on political economy. He has been an occasional adviser to Ministers and his articles have appeared in, among others, The Times, Financial Times, Daily Telegraph, Wall Street Journal and Guardian. He has frequently commented on political and economic affairs on radio and television. His two previous books "Government against the People" published in 1986 and "The Emancipated Society" published in 1988 were highly praised both in Britain and in the United States.

Introduction

There are two basic philosophies of Government: those systems which depend on political control and collective responsibility or those which rely principally on economic decentralisation and individual freedom. The political/collectivist systems can operate in the name of a religion or ideology or at the behest of a monarch or dictator. Despite the claims of the political collectivists to emancipate the people, history has shown them to be even more tyrannical than the rule of despotic individuals. Indeed the political collectivist systems usually raise their leaders to the kind of God like status which is a prerequisite for absolute tyranny – Ho Chi Minh, Stalin, Hitler, Pol Pot were all highly individualistic leaders of collectivism. Such systems permit neither individual democratic choice through elections nor individual economic choice through the operation of markets. Rather the power of the State grows inexorably as the freedom (and even identity) of the individual citizen declines.

The systems of Government which are ostensibly based on the capitalist market and Parliamentary Democracy may in theory at least provide a minimal State provision, emancipating the individual and his family from poverty and the arbitrary injustice of political collectivism or economic laissez faire. But too often such "democratic" systems have shared the attitudes of political collectivists and aped their State centralism and ideological controls.

For frequent elections based on universal individual franchise are no guarantee that the individual has even political influence, much less economic and social freedoms. Indeed it is through the ballot box itself that the individual's freedom of action is converted into the State's universal control.

Too often the belief in the justice of what free people *do* is confused and superseded by the assumption that Government should do what the people are deemed to have "decided". Too often the universal power which the people have delegated to Government for the performance of certain collective tasks is used to override the people's will in other areas. Too often the State "administration" of society overrides the Rule of Law and substitutes arbitrary power, making the infantile claim that virtually all the freedoms of the individual can be the subject of majority voting.

The State which is charged with the protection of rivers and beaches also owns and regulates the water companies which are the principal polluters of rivers and beaches. The State in Britain took over the health service and the coal, steel, nuclear and electricity industries which continuously poisoned the atmosphere and endangered – unchecked – the lives of its citizens. The State which claims to be the best educator of the underprivileged has achieved, in some areas of the United Kingdom, literacy levels equivalent to those in the workhouses of the 1840's.

And yet, despite their many failures there is an implicit assumption by all political parties that most social and economic problems have been caused by others and can be rectified by the State. The essays in this book demonstrate that the opposite is usually the case and that economic efficiency and democratic accountability are most often associated with Government withdrawal. Outside the emancipating roles of the State in welfare and "public good" provision – many of which should naturally reduce if successfully applied – the vast majority of social and economic decisions can and must be taken by individuals, families, responsible corporations and other free associations of responsible citizens. Where the State intervenes, controls, subsidises and takes over responsibility then economic progress, social accountability and individual learning and self improvement are redundant.

The State does not only act directly to promote its own interests and protect the privileges of its employees and agencies. Far more social leverage is achieved through financial allowances and legislative privileges for those able to lobby the offices of the State. Corporations, Trade Unions, professional associations, State industries and many financial sectors receive special treatment – payed for of course by the ordinary voter and taxpayer, blissfully ignorant of his sacrifice and tragically impotent to challenge the Government which claims to represent him. Democracy begins and should end with the individual. Government and the institutions of the State may, in limited spheres and with due modesty and accountability, be a *pillar* of Democracy but they cannot constitute the *totality* or even the majority of democratic activity. Too often the "Democratic State" takes on the powers and privileges which the people more readily associate with the trappings of dictators.

3

Usually these powers lead to increasing poverty and dependence, doing no more than widening the scope of privilege and patronage and concentrating power rather than removing and dissipating State controls.

This book describes the failure of Government activity, demonstrating how the State and the politics of power have very little to do with democracy and the freedom of the people.

There is no need for a total rejection of the State. Indeed there is a danger that excess State control could rebound towards a Laissez Faire agnosticism or – equally dangerous – a combination of capitalist freedom and State domination. Such a fatal combination (prevalent in Hitler's Germany and Mussolini's Italy) is now threatened in the United Kingdom with wealth and freedom for the majority based on the ability to join State and corporatist powers while the responsible individual or unorganised unemployed, willing to be accountable to their fellow citizens, are crushed between organised business or labour and the manipulative State. This process is made more probable in the UK by the embryo "Euro State" as it jockeys for a share of corporatist power in what is misleadingly called the "single market".

It is in the hope that these dangerous developments can be recognised by the electorate and those who "pragmatically" administer our economic and political institutions that I offer these essays on the democratic costs of Government.

PART ONE

The Politics of Economics

1 The Changing Map of Politics

Margaret Thatcher and the "new right" intellectual revolution
have undoubtedly changed the political map of Britain. The old
certainties of socialist left and capitalist right have been thrown
into doubt. Conservatives are split between paternalists and
libertarians. The centre parties are split between collectivist
liberals and individuals styled after one leader, David Owen.
The Labour Party is divided between state socialists and those
emphasising individual freedom.

From these conflicts within all of Britain's parties, it is easy to
see how archaic the old left-right-centre labels have become. Is it
"left wing" to challenge the State? Then the libertarian right is
left wing. Is it left wing to empower the consumer over the
producer? Then the market economist is on the left, not the
right. Is it right wing to concentrate power and defend the status
quo, where labour's relationship to the State is as a slave to its
owner? Then the world's socialist governments are not just
right-wing but totally reactionary.

The left-right political axis is now largely redundant – it is the
vertical axis authoritarian-libertarian which more truly reflects
public preferences. In the United Kingdom, even after eight
years of anti-state, pro-market economics, the left-right political
choice would cut the vertical axis above the midpoint – that is
toward the authoritarian end. But the paternalists, centralists
and collectivists in all political parties are on the defensive. As
class distinctions blur and the individual, regardless of social and
economic background, demands the freedom to accept responsibility for his money (lower taxes), his family (home ownership),
his job (no trade unions), and social provision (less state control

5

of education and health), then political parties based on collective interests must give way to those promoting individual freedom.

The individual rightly thinks his own responsibility and the competition of his fellow citizens are more democratic, direct and efficient constraints on his behaviour than the control of the State. Where private ownership in a competitive market has provided more wealth and given consumers more control than state ownership, where non-unionised workers are often more wealthy than the unionised, the distinction between capitalism and socialism is less obvious. Where the principal polluters of the environment are state-owned coal, steel, nuclear and electricity and state-run sewerage, what has socialism to offer?

Privatisation of major state industries has returned ownership to the people as shareholders. It has not, however, generally returned real "control" of the assets to the consumer through a competitive market. The challenge of justifying ownership of assets and the right to profit (so long as competitors allow) is the democratic essence of the capitalist market. The producer of a profit is "taxed" by his competitors and free consumers. But a Conservative government, having fostered increased competition, cannot then continue to levy taxes and spend the more than 40% of gross domestic product that constitute the British government's expenditure to "aid" those already benefiting from increased wealth in the marketplace.

The British government has now understood that market principles can be extended to the public sector provision of health and education services. The State and its employees and agencies should not be allowed to define the service the people require, dictate its form of provision and its cost, and then justify the status quo by writing their own reports of their "public service."

Vouchers for health care and education give consumers power to discipline public sector producers. Poor schools, teachers, doctors and hospitals must respond to the discipline of public choice, and good schools etc. must expand. The difficulty arises as to how the relationship between paying for the private sector and free public sector is allowed to develop. Generally, as a society becomes richer and more middle class we would expect the value of education and health care to be reflected in more and more people paying for that value themselves.

The State may have many functions today but, like any other

body claiming to be of service to citizens, it may no longer be required tomorrow. Those who work in state institutions cannot be given unlimited contracts and blank checks.

The State is democratically justified where it acts to represent all in certain collective tasks or where it emancipates the individual from conditions for which direct responsibility for his actions is not a fair reward for failure (youth, poverty, ignorance, addiction). These collective and emancipating roles must however contract as public need declines. Where the State exceeds these limits it takes on interests of its own and adopts increasingly *controlling* roles. The State becomes capable of doing what democracy should prevent *any* agency from doing – dictating the terms according to which the agency will be "successful."

Why, after so much state "help" does the State continue to expand and the assets controlled by the people it has "helped" decline? More state control has not led to less crime, fewer suicides, less unemployment but to greater licentiousness. This is because the very power of the State, designed to control the individual, guarantees him the conditions for irresponsible license. As state control grows there arise ever more violent forms of individual "deviation" from social norms – absentee-ism, demonstrations, emigration, strikes, black economy, theft.

Left-right, or capitalism-socialism, no longer characterise the conflict between the individual and the State. The relevant opposition is between emancipated and dependent societies. The dependent society is based on collectivism, State control and patronage, covert agreements and subservience to author-ity. The emancipated society is based on individual freedom, overt social signals, competition and "social challenge" to wealth and political authority.

The increased power which the emancipating roles of the State have given individuals can only be realized through the market place – that expression of public choices, the source of individual freedom, the justification of property rights, the creator of wealth and the prime mover in its dispersal. No wonder the State has always viewed the marketplace with suspicion.

The State prefers the power of taxation and the patronage of subsidy. But competition is the people's tax – it is efficient, not manipulable, and has no "collection" costs. Centralists and

7

collectivists in all parties are worried about such ideas for as the State is reduced to its legitimate roles democracy may become in practice what government would prefer remained a theory.

2   Ask a silly question...

"When did you stop beating your wife, Dr. Owen?"

Being that relative rarity among modern politicians, a man of some intellect, Dr. Owen would reply "Why would you or any other intelligent person, ask such a question?" On this response I would congratulate him but go on to quote from his party's "Opinions Questionnaire" of which I, along with many thousands of others, have received an unsolicited copy. "Do you believe" runs one of the questions, "that allowing unemployment to stay at current high levels is an acceptable way to hold down inflation?" Why, I ask, would any intelligent person ask such a loaded question? More important, what would he assume about the knowledge of the person to whom the question is addressed? For although the politician is perfectly happy without the encumbrance of relevant knowledge, responsible individuals are more comfortable with a smattering before giving their views.

The options questionnaire is, theoretically, a praiseworthy attempt to solicit political opinions in order, one assumes, to formulate policy. Most of the questions offer multiple choice answers. For instance "Should social security spending be (a) increased (b) decreased (c) no change." There is a helpful "pie chart" to illustrate the slice of Government income devoted to each sector of public expenditure. There is of course no attempt to illustrate *how* money is spent at present and whether it produces any goods or services of value for society. There is no attempt to explain the relationship between more money and better service or to ask what in the opinion of "the people" would *represent* good service. Nor are voters asked how they prefer to pay for or consume these services (taxes, personal expenditure, tax allowances, vouchers). Furthermore does "an increase in social security" mean that everyone receives more or that more receive the same amount? or will more money go to those who administer the social security system? or perhaps there will be an increase in their numbers?

The same question and multiple choice answer format covers other areas of Government activity – housing, law and order, health services – now there's an interesting definition! Do they mean health preservation like water, housing and sanitation or do they mean "illness services" like hospitals, doctors and medicines?

The problem with all Governmental decisions and the primitive analysis on which they are based is that there is an implicit assumption that either the people are incapable of making decisions for themselves and that therefore Government should do so on their behalf or that the people do know what they want but must articulate those needs in *words* so that the Government can *act* on their behalf. But it is beyond the ability of any Government to even grasp the complexities of the many and diverse preferences and choices made in society never mind accommodate them through centralised political decisions.

The SDP questionnaire perhaps says less about the policies of that party and more about the general approach to politics by all political parties. Indeed Dr. Owen as an individual has shown a healthy cynicism for simplistic social definitions and the effectiveness of Government activity and has shown signs of being prepared to trust the responsible actions of the people rather that the grandiose decisions of Government.

It is one of the strengths of Parliamentary Democracy that the more immediate, necessarily ill informed, reactions of the voters are filtered through their representatives. MP's are not delegates, nor, ideally, are MP's *representative of* the electorate. Rather they should represent voters' opinions and feelings when they are framing and enacting legislation.

There is an increasing tendency to demand the immediate translation into Government action of the results of scientifically dubious "opinion polls". For example much is made of the "opinion poll" support for the National Health Service. But would that support be forthcoming if the NHS were more accurately called the Nationalised Sickness Service or if the question were prefaced by the description of NHS waiting lists, avoidable deaths, incompetent surgeons and poor record on preventative medicine? Since at any given time 70% of the population has never used the NHS (except for the occasional pill prescription) should not the 30% who have be questioned? Would "the people" be so content if they actually knew what they were paying for the service? What if the conditions and health statistics of other countries which do not have a State health service or of those countries, like the USSR, which do, were known in detail?

The final question in the SDP questionnaire asks if the elector will make a contribution "to support our efforts" yes or no is hardly an adequate choice. For if "our efforts" mean more of the people's money being spent by politicians and therefore less by the people themselves doubtless those same people may wonder why they are being consulted. If on the other hand "our efforts" means a reduction in the role of Government and returning more economic and social decisions to the people then actions speak louder than political exhortations or Parliamentary motions. Vouchers for social choice are more potent than an opinion questionnaire.

But such radical ideas for a "people's choice" democracy somewhat cramp the style of paternalist politicians of all parties. Being employed to carry out *only* those necessary and relatively mundane activities which the people cannot better achieve without Government is not quite the glorious state of power over a deferential electorate that the politician had in mind.

Despite the promise of a radically liberal approach to democratic power the SDP seems to be tarred with the same corporatist brush as the other parties – except that centralised levers will be pulled by civil servants and teachers rather than Trade Unionists or Bankers. The "centre" of British politics makes Mrs Thatchers Conservatism look like radical liberalism. But wait . . . that is exactly what it is!

3   Mrs Currie's unhealthy Geordies

In a society in which working class resentment and inverted snobbery have for so long been the staple diet of politics it is not surprising that a Conservative Minister should be criticised for linking poor health with personal diet. Are we not used to finding the comfort of "social" (or usually socialist) explanations for our ills and political justifications for the most irresponsible of human actions?

Edwina Currie claimed that poor health in the North East, as detailed in a recent medical report, was not due to high unemployment but was at least in part due to poor eating habits and excessive drinking and smoking.

Is there any support for this view in the mass of social statistics which are compiled on a regional basis? If we compare the North with the richest area of the country, the South East, average earnings are about 15% lower. And yet we find that an equal or a higher percentage of Northern families possess washing machines, refrigerators and colour televisions than do families in the South East. Lack of money therefore hardly seems a reasonable explanation for poor health in the North.

% of households with certain durable goods

	washing machine	refrigerator	colour TV
North	79%	93%	83%
South East	74%	96%	82

The North has one of the highest levels of heart disease in Britain and a brief look at the typical Geordie's diet suggests that this is perhaps not surprising. Once again comparing the North's diet with that of the typical household in the South East we see that the Northerner consumes 10% more butter, 40% less fresh fruit, less vegetables, 12% more cake and 5% more sugar.

Even more significantly the typical Northern household spends 28% more of its income on alcohol and 42% more of his income on cigarettes than a typical household in the South East.

Household consumption of certain foods: ounces per week

	Butter	Fresh fruit	Cake	Sugar	Vegetable
North	3.4	21.1	9.9	11.4	44
South East	3.1	34.6	8.8	10.8	46

Household expenditure on alcohol and tobacco as a percentage of weekly expenditure

	Alcohol	Tobacco
North	6.1	4.0
South East	4.4	2.3
England	4.8	2.8

There is therefore considerable evidence to back up Mrs Currie's claim that the average Geordie's lifestyle is not exactly the healthiest in the country.

But perhaps the most objectionable aspect of the controversy has been the Labour Party's virulent personal attacks on Mrs Currie. Had she attacked Geordies? Of course not – at least no more than a doctor "attacks" his patient when he "accuses" him of being ill! But Socialists have never been interested in the welfare of the individual worker, his personal development and increasing independence. Socialism requires dramatic generalisations about "the working class", heroic images of poverty imposed by capitalsim and a *permanent* mass of dependent workers gratified for the occasional crumb from a table usually laden with socialist tracts and composite motions.

Conservatives on the other hand prefer to see an increasingly educated and independent "worker" joining the ranks of the middle class. The first step in this process is an honest diagnosis of the problems. Mrs Currie is more likely to provide that than socialists in search of ideological cannon fodder.

Of equal importance when considering such cases of public health and their causes and cures is to what extent the National Health Service is performing its proper role of preserving public health rather than just treating illness. Indeed how can the institution which regards hospital expansion and a large doctor and nurse payroll as a sign of its "success" have an incentive (never mind a Government defined duty) to reduce illness?

A large private sector health provision/illness treatment service would have a strong incentive to balance the need for eg a new hospital with increased spending on preventive medicine. A similar process can be observed in the USA where electricity utilities install free energy conservation equipment in order to reduce the need for investment in more power stations. In the UK we have witnessed in the Agriculture Ministry an inability to represent both consumer health concerns and farmer interests while the other ingredients of public health – education and water quality – are bureaucratically separated from the Ministry of Health.

The most important element in a society which preserves freedom is the need for individual responsibility to replace State control wherever possible. The first step towards that responsibility is self knowledge – that is sufficient awareness of one's own condition to act on one's own initiative to improve that condition. It is not surprising that it was a Conservative Minister, valuing individual freedom and responsibility, who warned and informed the people of danger. Nor was it a surprise to see such a process of individual emancipaiton condemned by socialists and collectivists.

4   Now is the pen and ink of our discontent

People don't write letters to British Rail every time they have a complaint. Such behaviour would lead rapidly to the deforestation of the planet. However, as a token registration of my life long frustration with BR I did once write a letter.

It had been a journey of predictable disaster – the usual litany of incompetence, shoddy service and the feeling of any customer of a nationalised industry – that one's intrusion on the quiet life of an institution run for the benefit of its employees, was deeply resented.

I never kept a copy of my letter detailing BR's catastrophic attempts to perform the simple operation of conveying me from Newcastle to London. It was an everyday story of simple BR folk – train left late and arrived late, buffet car had no food, no station toilets available, carriage freezing, usual acrid rotten eggs smell when the 125 braked and the usual health hazard from sitting smokers next to non smokers. The latter is symptomatic of the plodding thought processes of BR – the idea that non smoking compartments are for people who don't want to smoke. Even London Transport have grasped the simple truth that they don't want to *breathe* smoke!

As befits the slow grinding logic of a monopoly unresponsive to market forces the reply to my letter was a detailed point by point *description* of (but little apology for) the abject list of failure. The immaculate logic made hilarious reading. The train had left late because it had been delayed. It had arrived late because it had left late. The brakes smelled because they usually did when applied at high speed. The carriage was cold because the heating system was (inexplicably) not functioning properly! There was the usual arrogant insistence that non smokers were adequately catered for.

On a more recent occasion the tale of incompetence resembled a Brian Rix farce. Three times between Oxford and Newcastle, three different guards took over without being informed by the previous duty guard that the air conditioning in one of the carriages was not functioning. On a hot day it was merrily roasting the hapless – and for the most part uncomplaining – passengers. Each guard turned on the defunct air conditioning, eventually detected that 100 degrees was even by British Rail's criteria, not comfortable ambient temperature for rail travel, and then turned it off again. Until your long suffering chronicler of these events rose to threaten the third guard with death or a holiday travel pass on British Rail unless he turned the damned thing off, the most remarkable British phlegm (or is it just supine indifference?) had allowed the ludicrous situation to pass without comment.

This surely is the real reason for the "British disease" as our Continental friends call our slow and inexorable decline. We really are such a nice uncomplaining lot. Never object to the service we pay for – goods, travel, hotel, food. "Mustn't spoil our holiday by making a fuss!") Bad buyers create bad products and the British are surely the worst buyers in the world. Witness the American complaining about the quality of goods or hotel service. Witness the Frenchman or German sending back food in a restaurant or calling out their comments on a poor film at the cinema. It is such feedback which stimulates producers and suppliers to better service. Indeed such responses show that the customer is in possession of any vital signs at all and not just a passive putty-like poltroon to be exploited by those who should serve him and treated with contempt by those who should respect him.

The dumb, lackadaisical acceptance of failure in our society has been so well exemplified in those who represent their country in our major sports. Bob Willis, about to retire from England's cricket team recognised that our cricketing failure was due to an attitude of mind, encouraged by lack of competition for places in the team.

> "This bred a natural complacency, subconscious or not and I find it disturbing to see how readily many of the blokes accepted a poor performance or a bad result and how quickly they resigned themselves to defeat and forgot about it. This is an English trait which I can find little to commend."

How typical this has been of the entire British economy, how redolent of the non competitive environment in which the Nationalised Industries go about their sullen exploitation of consumers, how typical of Trade Unionists confident of their monopoly position and immune from the embarassment of competition from those outside their closed shop.

16

What are the consequences of this trail of commercial irresponsiblity throughout British life? As one might expect from a confrontation with the hegemony of non commercial waste, the people are forced to resort to equally wasteful methods to combat it. Letter writing is the consumer's pathetic response to monopoly exploitation by nationalised industries for whose incompetence he pays in excessive prices, poor services and subsidies paid out of his taxes. Not surprisingly in the Russian communist system unconstrained by free consumers a British writer found Soviet journalists enjoying "surprising leeway" and "writing long pieces about particularly flagrant examples of pollution, economic mismanagement and corruption". God help the society whose economic efficiency can rely *only* on the investigations of journalists.

The collective equivalent of journalism and letter writing is political pressure through Parliament to influence the actions of State industry. Both these responses lack transparency, are slow, easily corruptible and rely on the same avenue of political power which those same industries are far more adept at using.

How far this is from the democracy and efficiency of the market place where competition and private ownership allow the consumer to be the master. It requires no Government leglislation, consumers committees or thousands of letters to GEC or Marks and Spencer for an improvement in customner service. The consumer cracks the whip and the commerically constrained come running.

The day is approaching when British Rail and, who knows, even Postal and Health industries may be toppled from their protected, gilt edged thrones by triumphant consumers and thousands like myself can throw away the pen and ink of our discontent.

5   Trade Union Monopolies

A recent Monopolies and Mergers Commission inquiry into working practices in television and film industries focused attention once more on the Trade Union closed shop. When relatively unskilled production assistants in television can earn over £25,000 per annum, an investigation was long overdue.

The Government's industrial relations legislation since 1979 has concentrated on eliminating "secondary action" and on "returning the unions to their members" through increased secret balloting. But asking members of a closed shop to vote on its continued existence is like asking shareholders in a company whether they wish to remain a monoploy.

To permit a Trade Union to control and sell its members through a closed shop and exclude from employment those who will not join what is usually a highly political union would be unacceptable even if some general good arose. But can even this mitigating claim be justified? Do closed shops always give workers power or does it depend on the structure and ownership of their industry?

Throughout the 1960's and 1970's the percentage of workers in closed shops grew considerably but since 1980 traditionally unionised industries – like engineering, textiles, coal and printing have declined while jobs have increased in sectors where unions were weak – for instance in professional services, banking, catering, hotels. Television companies have both grown in employment and maintained extensive closed shop provisions – a relative industrial rarity.

But how successful are closed shops in defending their members jobs and increasing their pay? These two criteria were weighted equally in a study of the closed shop in my recent book** Statistics cover 15 different Standard Industrial Classifications with the minimum percentage of workers in closed shops ranging from 87% (in mining and quarrying) to 5% (in miscellaneous services) as determined by a London School of Economics study.

Points were awarded for relative success in maintaining employment between 1978 and 1982 and in achieving wage rises

**The Emancipated Society (1988)

18

between 1976 and 1982. These years cover short and roughly equal periods of modest growth, boom and recession respectively and therefore offer a reasonable assessment of Trade Union ability to represent their members in very different economic circumstances. The total score was an attempt to assess the connection between success in maintaining employment and wage levels and the degree of union control through the closed shop.

However, worker success in these matters is not solely due to the power of the closed shop but often, more importantly, to the commercial constraints on the industry with which unions are bargaining. An industrial sector dominated, as mining, by a government financed monopoly is able, by passing on costs to captive consumers and taxpayers, to accommodate the demands of its monopoly union bargainers with some ease. Other characteristics which are in effect "subsidies" to Trade Union effectiveness are high industrial concentration and low import vulnerability. In my study the success of the closed shop in achieving higher wages and maintaining employment was adjusted for the effects of the "subsidies" on the different industrial sectors.

The importance of import penetration for trade union bargainers was demonstrated in the shipbuilding/marine sector. A 57% closed shop did not prevent high job losses and modest earnings since in a declining industry there were few barriers to the import of ships as existed, for instance, in the import of coal during this period.

In the private sector, industrial concentration is of prime importance for Trade Union effectiveness. High concentration in the private sector is usually the result of high barriers to entry, many of which are constructed and strengthened by Trade Union power. The paper printing and publishing sector is a classic example of where high concentration of ownership (often subsidised by rich individuals) has permitted effective Trade Union closed shops.

Making allowances for industrial structure there seems to be no connection between closed shop coverage and worker success in maintaining employment and wage rises. Some of the highest levels of closed shop coverage – shipbuilding and metal manufacture – have the lowest success ratings while sectors with the lowest closed shop coverage – insurance, banking, electrical engineering and miscellaneous services – have the highest scores. Although unions may be able to take advantage of the closed shop to extract maximum utility at any point in time, the power to do so will also tend to prevent change and long term prosperity in that industry as coal, docks and shipbuilding have proved.

Had the petroleum products market for instance not been vulnerable to imports and had it enjoyed the protection of the public purse, as for example the coal industry, the 55% closed shop would have maintained employment levels and prevented investment in higher value capacity – but only at the cost of long term prosperity for that sector.

The following conclusions can be drawn about the strength of the closed shop in promoting the interests of workers:

- There is no connection between the strength of the closed shop in an industrial sector and the defence of jobs and wage levels.
- The stronger the closed shop the more workers will be able to achieve higher wage levels but the less they will be able to preserve employment.
- In the short run workers in strong closed shop sectors which are protected by State monopoly and import controls, can be as successful as those in growth sectors with low closed shop coverage.
- In the longer run the most successful workers will be in growth industries where the closed shop does not exist or has low coverage.
- The closed shop can be effective only where forces are operating to protecting the employer: low import vulnerability, public sector ownership, monopoly or high industrial concentration.

It is little wonder that the highly concentrated, partly public funded, import protected television industry should be the object of an inquiry by the Monopolies and Mergers Commission. But did not the Government itself establish and protect this industry from which the Trade Unions now derive such benefit? Quis custodiet ipsos custodes?

It may well be the effects of satellite television, more terrestrial channels and the obligation to buy in 25% of programming which will most severely limit Trade Union protectionism. The MMC inquiry has not even proved a condemnation of past ills, the Government's referal being no more than a public expression of its dissatisfaction with its own activities. As usual the real moves towards economic democracy and consumer choice will come not from a handwringing Government "doing something" but through the people acting freely where the Government previously controlled.

6   Why Import Gas?

In 1984 the then State owned British Gas Corporation was about to conclude a contract with a consortium of (non British) oil companies to buy, over many years, the gas from the Sleipner field in the Norwegian sector of the North Sea. Shortly after the author published the following paper the Government prevented the Corporation from signing such a contract. The result was a very large balance of payments saving for the UK economy, the enhancement of the UK's own gas reserves and a boost to British offshore oil companies. The Sleipner affair is a vivid demonstration of the economic effects of State monopoly and non market pricing.

The Sleipner gas field is located in the Norwegian sector of the North Sea. The 7 trillion (million million) cubic feet of gas it contains have been the subject of negotiation between the British Gas Corporation (BGC) as potential purchaser and the participants in the field consortium (all non Biritsh oil companies). Within United Kingdon waters there are, according to Government estimates before the recent revival in gas exploration, 33 trillion cubic feet of gas yet to be recovered.

British Gas Corporation already imports some 25 percent of the United Kingdom's gas supplies from the Norwegian sector of the Frigg field and seeks to replace these supplies, as Frigg production declines in the early 1990's, with gas from the Sleipner field. The total cost over the life of the field to the United Kingdom, at today's prices, would be £20,000 million.

Because the United Kingdom has prevented the export of gas, the monopsony of the British Gas Corporation has always paid higher prices for imported gas than it has been prepared to pay for domestic gas. This has meant encouraging gas exploration and production in the Norwegian sector and discouraging exploration and production in the UK sector. The "need" to import then becomes a self-fulfilling prophecy. Not only has this meant a large import bill but there has been no way of balancing these imports since gas exports have been prohibited. The BGC purchase of Sleipner gas would continue and exacerbate this state of affairs.

The British Gas Corporation's decision to pursue Sleipner gas purchase and its pricing of domestic gas are based not on commercial responsiblilty but on the Corporation's position as a powerful monopsonist in relation to oil companies operating in the UK, a de facto monopolist supplier of gas to UK consumers and a Government agency operating in effect with State subsidised capital (i.e. its pricing is based on the fact that the shareholder has not required market returns on his capital and can therefore undercut the private sector).

There must be serious doubts about the basic price and supply assumptions underlying BGC's interest in Sleipner gas and the general lack of commercial constraint on the Corporation. We therefore urge the Secretary of State for Energy to consider the following costs for the UK as a whole of the import of Norwegian gas from the Sleipner field:

1. A very large loss of tax revenue for the UK Government. Incremental revenues could be £500 million per trillion cubic feet of developed reserves in the UK.

2. The loss of many onshore jobs plus profit opportunities. British Petroleum have estimated that 700 jobs will be generated directly from the development of four small gas fields.

3. A *huge* balance of payments burden well into the 1990's when our own energy earnings will be declining. The annual commitment of £1.5 billion compares with the UK's current account surplus of £2.0 billion in 1983. A commitment of this size is bound to have a depressing effect on sterling, which in turn will increase the sterling price of gas, since the Norwegians will have effectively linked the gas price to the US dollar.

4. UK funds will produce high returns to the Norwegian Government, and foreign investors in foreign gas fields rather than returns to the British Government and UK operators in the North Sea.

5. Using tax payers' money to perpetuate the very BGC stranglehold on the gas industry the results of which now cause them to panic about UK supplies.

6. There are many signs that Europeans are not interested in the rigid Norwegian gas contracts nor their prices. They would therefore not be interested in UK exports at prices which would allow a net return to the UK if Sleipner imports were counteracted by UK exports.

7. If the high price of Sleipner gas suppressed UK gas demand then it is UK suppliers, not Sleipner owners, who will suffer

23

cut backs, to the detriment of UK tax revenue, profits and jobs.

8. By committing to long term imports of Sleipner gas the UK also stifles the commercial development of gas from our substantial coal resources and thereby reduces the coal industry's potential contribution to the nation's wealth.

The Sleipner contract will not help the UK by "keeping UK gas in the ground". Firstly because any general *rise* in gas value will be reflected in what we pay for Sleipner gas, thus cancelling any rise in the value of UK gas in the ground. Secondly, no resource has any value unless it is sold and the uncertainty of future values is greater than the certainty of today's sales price. Thirdly, UK platform builders and suppliers cannot exist merely to wait for a 1990's Shangri La.

Neither the Government, nor anyone else, can judge the BGC's "need" for more gas in the 1990's without seeing

1. The sales volume effects of recent higher consumer prices in the UK.
2. BGC gas price assumptions, oil price assumptions and coal price assumptions.
3. The effect on demand of passing to the consumer the Long Run Marginal cost implicit in the price offered for Sleipner gas.

A long term Sleipner contract would ease BGC's perceived supply problems and put BGC in a buyers market again. However, such a strategy has a high cost and has proved to have failed to produce market pricing and therefore adequate supplies in the past. In addition it would conflict with the Government's aim to rationalise and marketise the Energy sector in the interests of public finances and industrial investment.

In the gas, as in the electricity industry, the purchasing power of the public sector prevents rational private sector pricing and supply. Sleipner gas purchase will further jeopardise the ability of private sector supply in the UK since BGC, buttressed by new gas, can use average historical prices to under-cut new private sector gas. By taking higher priced foreign supplies and stifling cheaper domestic production the long term effect is higher consumer prices.

If the British Gas Corporation can commit £20,000 million of public money for the provision of gas supplies in competition with potential suppliers of Combined Heat and Power (CHP), the Government should offer the price per therm implicit in the Sleipner contract to the coal and electricty industries for CHP projects. They would then see a far better return on their investment.

The rise in demand for gas between 1973 and 1981 was not reflected in consumer prices nor in the prices paid by the British Gas Corporation for its supplies from UK operators. While total energy demand *fell* by 8 percent between 1977 and 1982, gas consumption rose by 2.4 percent while potential UK gas producers were receiving BGC pricing signals that indicated no rise in demand. The sudden change in recent BGC price offers comes at a time when consumer prices have risen dramatically and before the full implications for demand have really been registered.

The disastrous effects of the non market pricing of UK gas can be seen during the 1970s. As gas demand rose, in absolute terms and relative to total energy demand, exploration drilling in the principal gas area, East of England, fell as a percentage of total UK drilling from 16 percent in 1973 to 0 percent in 1978, 1979 and 1980. Gas development drilling fell from 100 percent of total drilling in 1973 to 0 percent in 1980.

There has been an unjustifiable discrepancy between prices paid for UK southern gas prices and prices paid for Norwegian Frigg and Ekofisk gas and for equivalent energy from oil. Little wonder that few new UK reserves are on offer to the British Gas Corporation. Not a single gas field in production today is less than 10 years old and the average is 17 years old.

The activities of the British Gas Corporation produced the ludicrous siutuation whereby the demand for a commodity rose consistently while the search for that commodity declined dramatically.

There must be considerable doubt about the long term demand for gas in the UK until recent price rises have had their effect on demand. However, even if demand were to remain stable, reserve levels would indicate a slow fall in supply to the United Kingdom to reach today's levels in about 1988 if only *existing* reserves in the UK southern, central and northern basins were brought on-stream.

The addition of Sleipner supplies would mean, by 1991, an increase of no less than 30 percent over existing UK supplies. In the light of demand uncertainties following recent prices rises in

25

the UK this planned increase in supplies would seem to be somewhat optimistic.

A consistent long-term policy of market pricing in the UK sector is likely to increase reserves dramatically and Sleipner gas could become unnecessary.

There is only one foolproof method of ensuring that such market pricing is consistently applied – UK operators must be free to export gas.

The Department of Energy has rightly asked the British Gas Corporation to consider the import of Dutch gas. Such imports, although not as good as stimulating UK domestic gas production, are in general going to be cheaper than Norwegian gas. In addition a pipleline constructed to import Dutch gas can also be used to import Soviet, Algerian *and* Norwegian gas as well as permitting UK gas exports to the Continent.

When considering long-term gas contracts in Europe BGC and the Department of Energy should bear in mind the recent comments of the Director of the Norwegian Institute of Petroleum:

> " ... the technical cost of Norwegian gas is much higher than that of Soviet gas or Algerian gas, making Norway the least supply elastic of the three major future suppliers to the west European gas market. Thus Norwegian gas is less competitive against coal or nuclear fuel than is either Algerian or Soviet gas."

Conclusion

It seems remarkable that a Government which prevents the free import of cheaper coal for the Electricity Supply Industry should permit the British Gas Corporation to under-price domestic gas and purchase more expensive supplies from abroad – a situation which Sleipner imports would perpetuate.

The Government should immediately permit the export of gas from UK, thus raising prices paid to dometic British gas producers to market levels. To allow time for domestic price rises to have their effect on domestic demand and for more UK supplies to become available, the option to import (smaller) amounts of Dutch gas should be considered, rather than commit to massive Sleipner gas imports.

However, the general principle of importing gas from abroad at prices in excess of domestic levels will continue to stifle the development of the United Kingdom's wealth and make us increasingly dependent upon foreign supplies. The overall costs of such a policy in terms of foregone income, jobs and foreign exchange have already been extremely high.

SUMMARY AND CONCLUSION

1. The British Gas Corporation, which already imports some 25% of UK gas supplies, is negotiating to buy, at a cost of £20,000m, gas from the Norwegian Sleipner field. The annual commitment of £1.5 billion compares with a 1983 current account surplus of £2 billion.
2. Because the United Kingdom has prevented the export of gas, the monopsony of the British Gas Corporation has always paid higher prices for foreign gas than it has been prepared to pay for domestic gas.
3. This has encouraged exploration and production in the Norwegian sector of the North Sea and discouraged exploration and production in the UK sector. The "need" to import more gas then became a self fulfilling prophecy! The BGC purchase of Sleipner gas would continue and exacerbate this state of affairs.
4. BGC's long term underpricing of gas to domestic producers over the last 10 years has brought about the ludicrous situation whereby increasing demand for a commodity coincided with a dramatic decline in the search for that commodity.
5. Allowing additional imports of gas in large volumes over a long contract period would re-establish the BGC stranglehold on the UK gas industry, the past results of which now cause a panic about future supplies. Uneconomic pricing has made it impossible to determine either true demand or true supply – both BGC and the oil companies are "groping in the dark".
6. It is illogical to allow the British Gas Corporation to import more expensive gas from abroad when the Electricity Industry is prevented from importing cheaper coal.
7. If the BGC can commit £20,000m of public money for the provison of gas supplies in competition with potential suppliers of combined heat and power, the Government should offer the price per therm implicit in the Sleipner contract to the coal and electricity industries for CHP projects where a better return to the taxpayer is likely to result.

8. There can be no economic case for importing gas in order to "keep UK gas in the ground" in the hope of future returns. UK platform builders and suppliers cannot exist merely to wait for a 1990's "Shangri La".

9. The BGC commitment to the Sleipner gas field would mean exporting job opportunities, foregoing corporate and Government revenue, financing foreign oil companies in foreign waters and benefiting the Norwegian Government in their search for Norwegian gas rather than the British Government in their search for UK gas.

Conclusion

10. Companies operating in the UK sector of the North Sea must be able to export gas freely. This would mean a rise in the price paid to UK operators and a chance for UK gas to be developed in competition with foreign gas. Real prices and a more transparent market would be established – without panic decisions based on distorted information from controlled prices in a politicised market. This can only be brought about by preventing, delaying or radically reducing the proposed import of Sleipner gas by the British Gas Corporation.

7 Economists and the Corporatist Economy

(A Book Review)

If you want to know about the study of economics, ask an economist. If you want to know about the economy he is the last person you should ask. What passes for an "economist" in Britain today is either employed by Government (directly in the civil service or indirectly in academic life) or is a journalist on one of the quality newspapers. Neither group are ever in danger of bearing financial repsonsiblity for their theories. Some are modest about their prescriptions and the ability of Government to act upon them efficiently. Others, like William Keegan – a devout and unreconstructed Keynesian – believe that economists "know" things because they have "seen the figures" and that "Government should be acting" on the basis of their theories.

On the cover of Keegan's book "Britain without Oil" there is a picture of a desolate "de-industrialised" landscape with an empty overgrown motorway winding its way between (non smoking) chimney stacks. The burden of the author's song is that this desolation awaits Britain "after the oil runs out" because Mrs Thatcher's wicked monetarists have destroyed British industry and have not used the revenues from North Sea Oil to invest in manufacturing industry.

When Keynesians talk of what "must be done" they do of course mean "Government must do... " In their simple world no jobs are created , no wealth made, no goods produced no Shangri La established without the intervention of Government – as investor, planner, educator, exchange rate manipulator and "demand creator". The entire vocabulary of post war Keynesians (oh for the healthy German attitude - praise Keynes and ignore the Keynesians) and the "tripartite consensus" corporatism which financed and subsidised their theories, is riddled with definitions and assumptions which any rational and responsible individual would have rejected in order to survive in the commercial world.

Keegan, not surprisingly, hardly quotes a single businessman but his book is full of the empty tautologies of Wynne Godley, NEDO and Lord Kaldor, not one of whom ever invested in a factory, financed stocks, produced goods or made a profit on their own account. Godley gives us such wisdom as:

> "... in the period 1967-78 the volume of exports of manufactured goods had risen by 50% every seven years but the volume of imports had risen by 100% every seven years".

or:

> "the balance of trade in manufacturing which had been in surplus throughout the previous two centuries has been in deficit since 1983.

There are no answers to questions like "Why do the British allow such things to happen?" "of what value is loss making manufacturing or loss making exports?" "Has there been any lack of Government intervention?" or "Has not Government intervention to disguise prices and true costs not brought about this very failure?". But no, the answers to these questions do not spring from the turgid prose of a University PhD, nor the neat symmetrical columns of Treasury statistics – they therefore fall outside the restricted purview of the "economist".

Like Godley, NEDO – that apotheosis of British corporatism – is quoted ad nauseam with such blinding insights as:

> "Faster expansion of manufacturing is to be expected when, in time, the exchange rate reflects the decline in oil revenues".

Brilliant! do we really need committees of the great and the good to tell us this? Why? Are they going to do something? If they are, they can use their unbounded wisdom to set up businesses and employ their fellow citizens on their own accounts, without the intellectual protection of a committee and the financial protection of tax extracted from the very people they claim to be "helping".

The activities of NEDO have always been suspect but Keegan himself helps to scupper this haven of committee discussion and "research".

> "Although the NEDO study was produced in 1984 ... much of the statistical data does not go beyond 1981".

Not one of the inefficiencies and bottlenecks which existed in 1960 when NEDO was founded to relieve them is not far worse 20 years later. Keegan's embarassing comments on their statistics is just one of the reasons why! In a particularly amusing passage the author claims there are "no obvious villains" at the root of the decline of the British economy.

"NEDO contains both industrialists and trade unionists as well as Government representatives: it does not point the finger at unions, employees or the Government".

We could hardly imagine a more succinct summary of the reasons for Britains decline than this patronising justification of the corporatist Establishment. To anyone but a British "economist" the symptoms of economic decline chronicled by Keegan in this book point unerringly to Government as the sole source of failure. No other institution in society can fail repeatedly in the service of its fellow citizens without suffering the direct financial consequences of its failure. Only Government can maintain and finance not only its own failures but those of its acolytes – and it does so by taxing the successful. Legal immunity for Trade Unions, tax allowances for industry, subsidy for nationalised industries, protectionism for domestic industry, money-printing to rescue banks, poor purchasing (on behalf of the people) of education and health services – every State measure to frustrate the consumer and protect producers from the consequences of their actions has been lobbied from all governments since the war. Beer and sandwiches at Number 10 or a 5 course lunch in the City all helped to oil the wheels of State patronage, "quangos" and "tripartite" committees. Anyone from another planet who had observed the rudiments of economic and social life on earth would assume that "tripartite" embraced producer, consumer and perhaps Government – but not in Britain. Here "tripartite" meant the deliberate exclusion of the consumer and the establishment of the absloute power of producers – in both the private and the public sectors. Their protection was more important than the service of the consumer. Ironically the producers sowed the seeds of their own destruction, for Government protection from the sovereignty of consumers today can mean complete commercial failure in the long run – although by then the Cabinet Ministers, Trade Union leaders and captains of industry concerned will be dispensing whiskeys and worldly wisdom in the House of Lords or perhaps in a higher and even more inaccessible place!

Keegan quotes a 1982 NEDO study (with statistics up to 1978!) and again fails to draw the obvious conclusion:

"there had been a trend for UK production technology to become more capital intensive and less technology intensive – ie labour saving but not innovative... (but)... mature ie capital rather than knowledge intensive products

31

are likely to face a larger range of competing substitutes than would new products and hence command lower returns per unit of output."

Despite the strained and contorted language we see that industry has been doing things which are against its long term interests. Why were they so illogical? Why, because Government had intervened to provide irrational signals. Government had introduced accelerated capital allowances on most kinds of capital investment. This was an artificial subsidy to capital investment per se, not long run profitable investment which might well have meant employing, instead, more skilled workers. But here too Government, by raising National Insurance contributions and passing onerous employment legislation had raised the costs of employing people just at the time that it had lowered the cost of employing machinery. This lunacy was then "balanced" by more Government job creation schemes and employment subsidies. (For a description of many years of British "countervailing intervention" see my own article in the Guardian March 1984 "Support that serves only to distort".)

Government fiscal distortions since the war have been at least as damaging to rational and responsible behaviour as State ownership. Why should individuals who are persuaded by tax allowances that life assurance, house loans and pensions are the best investments continue to invest in industry? Why should corporations for whom high taxation indicate that profits are socially unacceptable set out to serve their fellow citizens when those who fail the people are rewarded with Government subsidies?

There is a straightforward (although not simple) cause of the UK's decline – the increasing dominance of Government and its failure to respond to democratic choice. When Government oversteps its legitimate bounds as the servant of the people, providing only those goods which the people acting in free association could not supply, then it contradicts the people's choice – politically and economically. Each economic failure is seen as an excuse for more of the very Government intervention which caused that failure.

Keegan's book "Britain without Oil" contains all of the Keynesian economic vocabulary and concepts which even today are the staple diet of media, politicians, Government and economists.　They can no longer be used to counteract the intellectual arguments of what is misleadingly called the "New Right". Some examples:

Inflation is assumed to be a "rise in prices" – of for instance oil or coal. As the pound falls in value, higher import prices are assumed to be "inflationary". This is not so. Inflation is the depreciation of the value of the currency and hence a rise in the price of all commodities paid for in that currency. Price rises (of oil or imports) are a separate issue and are signal of a rise in demand or fall in supply. Similarly there is no such thing as "wage inflation" – only Governments create inflation. Without Government wage rises in one sector mean wage falls, or price rises or profit reduction elsewhere.

Energy shortage: there has never been, nor ever will be (given a free and competitive market) a shortage of energy. The appearance of a shortage can be created by Governments, cartels or monopolies. Between 1972 and 1974 and between 1979 and 1981 oil and other energy prices rose dramatically as a Government cartel of oil producers took advantage of excess (inflationary) demand in the industrial nations. Tighter monetary policy and rational conservation and fuel substitution in response to those temporary imbalances have now rectified matters. The ratio of world energy production to consumption was about the same in 1972 as it was in 1984 but today there is an excess supply because artificial Government inspired (and therefore wrong) price signals in the 1970's stimulated excess production in the 1980's. The price has therefore fallen below its normal level. If Governments had not intervened the violent and wasteful fluctuations in prices, costs, production and consumption would not have occured. The essence of a market (as opposed to a command economy) is that nothing happens suddenly since many buyers and sellers respond gradually to prices which automatically discount as far into the future as it is rational to go.

Fiscal squeeze: It is a myth propogated both by Keynesian critics and, ironically, Government ministers that the UK has suffered a fiscal squeeze since 1979 because the PSBR has been reduced and because Government spending has been radically "cut". Nothing could be further from the truth. Government spending as a percentage of GDP is higher than in 1979 while the size of the PSBR is, after the windfall of £10 billion of North Sea taxes, not quite the same measure as it was. Nevertheless after

33

allowing for land and asset sales the PSBR is also higher today (1986) than in 1979.

Monetary Squeeze and Unemployment: Here the Keynesian critics at least have some justification. There has been a monetary squeeze and real high interest rates have made life difficult for corporations. But why are interest rates so high in real terms? Partly this is justified by the successful attempt to reduce inflation and bring about rational investment decisions but much of the reason for the high interest rate and the resulting loss of jobs is due not to monetary policy (which merely makes borrowers pay real interest to previously exploited lenders) but rather due to Government overspending on "public investment" a wasteful welfare system and State apparatus. For a Keynesian to criticise high interest rates while he simultaneously demands higher Government spending and borrowing is the ultimate hypocrisy – unless of course he wholeheartedly embraces inflation and the decimation of the people's savings!

Reagan's deficit: The Keynesian argument is that the USA has created many jobs by adopting a Keynesian deficit strategy. Nothing could be further from the truth. The USA has not raised public spending to produce a deficit which they finance by printing money. Instead they have reduced taxes to produce a deficit which they have financed by a responsible monetary policy with very low inflation. To that extent Mr Reagan has shown more confidence in individual Americans' use of their own money while Mrs Thatcher has prefered to keep overall taxation high hence giving more resources to the very institution – the State – which has proved least competent in its spending and investment.

I would not wish William Keegan and others to stop criticising the Government – there is much to criticise. But the Keynesians really must get up to date. The real burden on society is not this Government but Government per se and Mrs Thatcher's Government has defended both consumer and voter from the overweening State. But that makes Mrs Thatcher's brand of Conservatism far too radical for the Keynesian Establishment. After all the removal of power from Government and returning it to the people means less power to the academic Establishment, the Trade Union, professional associations, the CBI and the Civil Service – all of whom employ "economists". Mr Keegan is luckier than most – at the Observer I believe he is employed by Tiny Rowland!

PART TWO

The North – South Divide

1 State Intervention and Regional Development

The following is based on the author's film report for Channel Four Televison's "Comment" Programme.

It has become the conventional wisdom of all political parties in the UK that industry in the poorer regions has been decimated by market forces and that Government should intervene to reverse industrial decline. A closer examination of the industrial history of the so called "peripheral regions" of the United Kindom would indicate that the opposite is the case.

Newcastle upon Tyne was the headquarters of the Newcastle Electricity Supply Company which was one of the world's leading electricity utilities in the early years of this century, producing the cheapest electricity in Europe and a leading innovator in electricity technology. NESCO built advanced factories to which it distributed electricity and to which it attracted many companies and industries, creating much wealth and employment in the Northern Region. As a private company it carried out the functions performed today by 4 State agencies – the North East Electricity Board, the Central Electricity Generating Board, English Industrial Estates and the Northern Development Company and it did so without taxing the region it was helping or the workers it was employing.

The Japanese owned Nissan car factory in Washington Co Durham has so far received Government grants of about £150m but since about 97 pence of every Government pound comes from taxing the North East in the first place, this process represents a strange kind of aid.

Japanese investment in the UK over the last 3 years has amounted to over $1.5m for every job created. That is a considerable sum and it demonstrates how profitable those jobs are for the investor. Why then should the British taxpayer – and especially not the poor North East Region – be subsidising that investment?

Historically State intervention has been as much about job destruction as job creation. Jarrow in the North East is famous for the 1930's march to London to protest at high unemployment following the closures of Palmer's shipyard. In 1851 when the entrepreneur Charles Palmer built his shipyard the town's population was 3000. By 1921, as a result of the success of his venture, the town had attracted a population of 35,000. But it was not market forces which closed Palmers, it was the State. A London based committee of Government, Bank of England and a cartel of shipyard owners "voted" Palmers out of existence.

The crude State organised "rationalisation" of the shipbuilding industry in the early 1930's was a direct result of the State's equally crude boost to economic activity in the late 1920's. Shipbuilding orders had risen suddenly and dramatically to unsustainable levels and the artificially created capacity had then to be arbitrarily reduced. As is usual with government inspired "rationalisation" the votes of the politically astute override the public service of the commercially responsible.

The site of the former Consett Iron Company in Co Durham is now a desolate waste ground. In the early years of this century this small town was the world's largest steel producer. Today the company which built Consett and provided thousands of jobs over 140 years, is gone. It survived so long as a private company because it was disciplined by shareholders and free consumers both in Britain and throughout the world. But in 1967, having been State owned from 1946 to 1957, the Steel Industry was once again nationalised and Consett again became a remote outpost of a State industry based in London. In 1980 the works were closed and nearly 5000 jobs disappeared overnight, leaving local unemployment at 30%.

When Government nationalises industries and raises taxes on companies and individuals the result is political decision making in London. the North, like other "peripheral regions" of the United Kingdom needs economic autonomy and the ability to retain its own wealth, not political hand outs from the State, largely paid for out of its own taxes.

These are some of the reasons why I and most of my friends no longer live in the North East. At best we shuttle like Nomads between Northern homes and southern pay packets as we chase the capital, employment and power which all governments have drained to the South.

2 DeLorean lessons for Regional Policy

The crushing criticism by the House of Commons Public Accounts Committee of the Government's involvement in the DeLorean fiasco has come at a time when other Government created and financed institutions, the mining industry and the dock labour scheme are so graphically illustrating the waste of the nations resources through the irresponsibility of political decision making.

Even allowing for the exceptional problems of Northern Ireland the tale of incompetence, gullibility and failure to heed professional advice which characterise the DeLorean affair the Committees Report is a quite breathtaking demonstration of the total inadequacy of politicians for the task of economic decision making.

Even the present Government, who must be applauded for bringing the DeLorean tragedy to an end shows, on occasion, a regrettable inclination to draw a categorical line between "social" and "economic" policy in its dealings with industry. It was Norman Tebitt no less who described regional policy as "social" and definitley not "economic". But is not this Government's entire economic policy, indeed political philosophy, based on the assumption that industrial investment decisions, if taken by unprotected, unsubsidised rational competitors will be automatically "social" if they are economic? The market economy accepts Government provision of public goods, social security and transitional reliefs but these pale into insignificance when we consider the massive public subsidy and tax reliefs which increasingly "fly by night" international (and domestic) corporations pocket in our regions on their way to greener pastures.

It is of course not only the public purse which is milked by mobile corporations, enticed to even greater foolishness by Government largesse. The greatest tragedies in the DeLorean affair are the smaller companies who were drawn into supplier over dependence on the instantly created white elephant and then equally discarded and bankrupted when the new "investors" moved on.

The national sense of grievance is more easily aroused against the foreign corporation but the British people have even more reason to condemn their own Government and industries. Whether it was new car factories, oil refineries or aluminium smelters in Scotland or the artificial preservation of steel mills and coal mines in Northern England and South Wales, private and public sector companies have been most adept at extracting public funds either to do what they intended anyway or what they should never have contemplated.

What Governments never seem to ask themselves is how these regions were ever wealthy enough in the first place to attract the populations which they now seek to subsidise in loss making dependence on the rest of Britain. What of the magnificent industrial achievements of the Clyde, Tyne and Mersey whose people are now cannon fodder in the rhetoric of both paternalists and socialists on their road (south) to Westminster? Those areas were the cradle of the world's first industrial revolution, and produced some of our greatest entrepreneurs. Swann, Parsons, Armstrong, Stevenson, Arkwright – all they had was their geographic position, ingenuity and the freedom to trade – very much in fact like the Hong Kongs and Singapores of the post war period. They created whole industries and, by comparison to the landed poverty and dependence which preceded them unparalleled wealth for their workers. The small town in Durham called Consett, which today suffers 27% unemployment after 13 years dependence on the nationalised steel industry and Government subsidy came to an abrupt end in 1980, was once the world's largest steel producer (in private hands).

What these regions did not have of course was a massive State apparatus directing investment in comercially unconstrained nationalised industries and "encouraging" through fiscal largesse the investment of private industry.

The Government must realise that their own decisions, taken in London are the most detrimental to the regions – pricing and investment in postal services, telecommunications, energy, roads, rail, travel subsidies. Even Government financed infrastructure is national in concept, as likely to drain a region or populate it with branch plants, as it is to support it.

Government should localise decisions, regionalise commercial life and stop subsidising the rich regions and their taxpayers. The Business Expansion scheme is only one of many examples of unintentioned bias against the regions.

Injections of regional aid through Government machinery rewards those who know the machinery, not the new entrepreneurs in the regions. Subsidy and allowances to industry controlled outside the regions allows loss makers to retain human skills, land, equipment and capital which would be better used by businessmen within the regions. funds injected often merely raise the cost of other resources out of the reach of local businessmen.

Government should give the regions their *regional* infrastructure and their people training and a chance to trade freely with unsubsidised competitors. They will reward Government with the independence and wealth which their forefathers achieved.

3 A return to the Regions

Regional Policy in the United Kingdom has its origins in 1934 when the Government, in response to the decline in basic industries like coal, steel, and shipbuilding designated South Wales, West Cumberland, the North East and West Central Scotland as special areas for Government assistance. There was a new designation of areas and an expansion of regional aid after 1945 and such policies reached their peak in the mid 1970's when no less than 50% of the workforce lived in areas which qualified for regional assistance.

Regional Policy was never conceived as a *permanent* policy for the Regions *per se* but rather as a *transitional* policy for *industrial change* and its social consequences. And yet for over 50 years these industries have been deemed "in decline". For over 50 years such policies have – by their own aims – failed. They have failed not just because they could do nothing to increase wealth and jobs but because they actually contributed further to the crises in those regions. Table 1 compares the regional figures for unemployment in 1933 and 1986. Both on the basis of absolute unemployment and the regional variation in unemployment the situation was of course worse in 1933.

Table 1

Region	Unemployed as a percentage of insured workers (January, 1933)	Region	Unemployed as a percentage of registered workforce (January, 1986)
London	14.2	South East	10.3
South-Eastern	17.0	East Anglia	11.5
South-Western	19.6	South West	12.9
Midlands	20.2	East Midlands	13.1
North-Eastern	29.8	West Midlands	15.8
North-Western	25.7	Yorks & Humberside	16.0
Scotland	30.2	North West	16.7
Wales	37.8	North	19.5
Northern	28.9	Scotland	16.4
		Wales	17.9
UK	23.4	Northern Ireland	21.6
		UK	14.1

Source: Armstrong & Taylor

Coefficient of Variation. (SD divided by the mean)	0.289		0.209

41

Nevertheless, considering the billions of pounds spent on regional policy over the last half century the difference in the regional unemployment variations between 1933 and 1986 is very small.

There is much confusion as to what the aims of central government intervention in regional economies should be. Do we aim to raise the GDP per head in the Regions? – in which case outward migration is no problem and should even be encouraged. Do we wish to raise employment in the Regions (a) for those already there or (b) for a smaller population? – in which case levels and GDP per head are secondary (for option b. outward migration would be encouraged.) If regional wealth is the aim then natural industrial developments will achieve that without Government intervention – except to remove barriers to the mobility of capital and labour. If maximum employment for the existing workforce is the aim then regional discrepancies in *wealth* (as measured by GDP per head) are likely to grow. Both Labour and traditional Conservative regional policies have been of this latter type and Table 2 shows the predictable results.

CHANGE IN UNEMPLOYMENT 1965–1985
CHANGE IN GDP PER HEAD 1971-1984

REGION	% UNEMPLOYED			100=UK (minus Continental Shelf) GDP PER HEAD		
	1965	1982	1985	1971	1891	1984
North	2.4	17.3	18.9	86	94	90
Yorks/Humberside	1.0	14.1	15.1	93	92	87
East Midlands	0.8	11.7	12.7	96	95	98
East Anglia	1.2	10.6	10.7	93	96	97
South East	0.8	9.5	9.9	113	115	117
South West	1.5	11.3	12.0	94	95	95
Wales	2.5	16.1	16.9	88	84	86
West Midlands	0.6	15.7	15.5	102	90	90
North West	1.5	15.7	16.3	95	94	96
Scotland	2.8	15.0	15.6	92	98	96
Coefficient of variation: (Standard deviation Divided by mean)	0.496	0.186	0.191	0.075	0.081	0.087

Source: Regional Trends

The regional variation in unemployment decreased between 1965 and 1982 but the increase in regional wealth variation over a similar period suggests that much of this "employment creation" was artificial and subsidy inspired. This decrease also coincided with a massive rise in overall unemployment. Between 1982 and 1985 unemployment variation increased while the variation in regional GDP per head has increased consistently since 1971. This latter measure is more significant and less manipulable than employment statistics. GDP per head is also a more significant indication of *long* term employment prospects.

Is the regional problem really *a development* problem – ie merely an adjustment to 100 or 200 year industrial and demographic cycles – which happens to have its worst effects in specific areas? Or is it an inherently geographic problem? Northern rural and service towns can and do flourish. Southern inner cities can and do fail.

Each type of economic and industrial change has a different time horizon. Prices change weekly, products can change every two or three years, companies decline and rise again over periods of 10 to 30 years. Industries however rise and decline over periods of 50 to 200 years and such basic industrial change is of a far higher order, affecting whole regions nations and continents. The basic industries built up by Britain in the 18th and 19th centuries (later taken up and developed by Europe and America) – steel, coal, shipbuilding – are in decline as alternative forms of energy, fabrication and transport become available and as developing countries with lower labour and raw material costs can extract more added value from these processes than Britain.

These industries were based around coal deposits and ports which were predominantly in the North of Britain. Their decline has produced – for all the exceptions and qualifications to the expression – a "North – South Divide".

The study by champion et al of 280 Local Labour Market Areas (LLMA's) gives credence to this basic delineation of the regional problem. One of the poorest LLMA's Corby is the nearest to London (some 120 miles) while "The best performing LLMA's all lie within the South East Standard Region".

Following the precipitate post war industrial decline in the United Kingdom, it was necessary after 1979 to "retrench" and it was inevitable that radical change would affect those regions of *historical* industrial success most of all. Indeed, it was also inevitable that having relied on Government subsidy of outdated industrial assets the poorer Regions of the United Kingdom would suffer a more dramatic collapse than those regions which had not received such extensive support. Equally it was to be expected that at first the efficiency of market forces would favour the South of England (where traditional manufacturing and extractive industries never dominated) and from where new growth, wealth and job creation would then permeate the peripheral Regions.

However this last step in national economic progress has been retarded by the continuation of Government distortions of the economy. The whole economic and political relationship between the Centre and the Regions must be re-appraised. This paper analyses the "Regional Problem" of the United Kingdom on the basis of the following themes:

1. When Government "spends money on the Regions" it raises taxation from the very regions it is claiming to help. The poor regions contribute 95% of their own aid.

2. Government Regional Development Grants have concentrated on mobile manufacturing plants – the very characteristics which correlate most strongly with industrial closures.

3. If the Regions continually look to the Centre for *social* support they use increasingly *political* means to do so, making themselves more and more dependent on London and the various Government institutions more easliy accessible to Southern based lobbyists.

4. Government intervention in the Regions is a *two way* process. High profile is given to inputs (i.e. Regional Development Grants) but little attention is given to outputs (i.e. national taxation or nationalised pricing or dividend payments). This is not just a question of *net* benefit or loss but, more significantly, from whom taxes are raised (internal wealth creators) and by whom funds are re-injected (external administrators).

5. Funds flow into a region is in the long run a question of a balance sheet of ownership. Taxes extracted from local equity owners and used as grants for external (often foreign) equity owners establish a long term drain of value added from the regions, cancelling out any Government support. ("Regional Equity Loss").

6. National fiscal policy and macro economic analysis often cut across and frustrate regional economic development. Similarly non fiscal measures such as housing, employment and Trade Union legislation can distort regional economies and prevent labour and capital mobility.

44

7. Market pricing allows the movement of goods and companies to replace the mass movement of people. If the market prices are controlled, distorted and subsidised at the Centre the mass migration from the Regions – or permanent unemployment – are inevitable.

There are those who, having identified the economic symptoms of the "North South Divide", are now proposing massive Government intervention in the Regions of Britain.

But given the history of regional economic support detailed in this paper a fresh round of intervention by central Government is unlikely to succeed. Indeed central Government's spending on the regions has not only failed to promote regional economic health, it would seem to have compounded those Regions' failure. Their industries have been artificially preserved, the skills of their employees either under utilised or exported, regional savings and investment distorted and the least affluent areas have failed to establish political and economic independence.

There is an alternative to this kind of intervention– a "market" alternative based primarily on Government withdrawal which could well be cheaper in the short term and more effective in the long term provision of wealth, employment and regional independence.

A NEW APPROACH TO REGIONAL POLICY

The very term "Regional Policy" is somewhat misleading, for central Government is interested not so much in the physical entity of the "Regions" but in the economic prospects of those who live there.

In Europe – where regional problems are traditionally agricultural rather than industrial – there is a more tangible connection between land and population but in the declining industrial centres of Glasgow, Merseyside and the North East Government Policy has been directed at job creation rather than land preservation and at subsidising and nationalising existing industrial assets rather than identifying the patterns of entrepreneurship and wealth creation which originally attracted those regions' populations.

It is interesting to note that the highest levels of unemployment are in the North, Wales and Northern Ireland – all areas where Government owned monopolies (steel, coal and ship-building) have dominated the local economy. Of the 20 poorest towns in the United Kingdom 7 are, or have been dominated by shipbuilding, 4 by coal mining and 7 by the steel industry. As nationalised industries have attempted to "save jobs" Government grants and allowances have been designed to "create jobs". But the concentration on mere employment (however politically attractive in the short term) is an ineffective policy objective since permanent jobs are not sustainable without a continuous process of wealth creation. Wealth creation in turn requires adaptability and commercial change arising from a sensitivity to customers needs. Where State monopolies abound the consumer is powerless to exert pressure on commercial shareholders by taking his custom elsewhere. The intervention of the State in industry (as opposed to welfare) prevents communication between consumers and producers and blunts those very social signals (costs, prices, interest, profits, losses) which identify problems and aid their resolution. Nationalised industries not only divorced the producer from the consumer but also the regional corporations and market from the new "owners" at the political centre – usually in London.

When this State isolation of business from consumers comes to an end the sudden job losses are devastating. Between 1976 and 1981 61% of the jobs lost by the top 10 job losing companies in the UK were shed by State owned corporations.

Although some steps have been taken to open up those markets where nationalised insustries still exist – electricity, coal and steel – many years of State industries' failure to produce commercial returns have severely distorted industrial investment – particularly in the regions and particularly in these industries.

There have always been many potential local energy initiatives (conservation investments, combined heat and power, hydro electricity etc.) which at commercial rates of return and in a competive market would have gone ahead to the benefit of regional economies and investors. But confronted by investment by State owned industries at low or even negative rates of return, they could never be realised.

Now that the Government has embarked upon an ambitious process of privatisation the steps which were originally taken towards nationalisation should in theory be reversed. However, there seems to be a desire to privatise monopolies rather than to re-create the regionally based competing corporations which were originally nationalised.

Before the first world war only 20 of the United Kingdom's top 100 companies had their headquarters in London. Today some 95% are based in London. There would be benefits if future privatisiations concentrated on decentralisation, regional competition and consumer power – not the maximum revenue for central Government while fiscal incentives which encourage institutional saving and investment – and hence centralised London based control of major corporations – should be reduced or eliminated.

This paper emphasises not what Government does or should do in the form of regional assistance but rather what it should *not* do. By encouraging such aid from the centre the regions have made themselves more and more dependent politically and economically on London and its various Government institutions (whether under Labour or Conservative administrations).

Despite this persistent failure (or perhaps *because* of such failure) there has grown up a plethora of Government tax reliefs, grants, "enterprise Zones" capital allowances and State financed agencies. This is partly financed by withdrawing from those very regions billions of pounds in the form of individual and corporate taxation, national insurance, road taxes and the non market pricing of coal, gas, electricity, water and telecommunications imposed and ultimately collected by a South East based bureaucracy. While taxes are universally applied to all regions, tax *allowances* (see below) favour the wealthier areas. Funds tend to be extracted from businessmen and workers who create wealth locally and distributed by civil servants who merely administer centrally.

It has frequently been noted that entrepreneurship is less evident among the regional "working class" than among South East based middle class accountants. This is not an *inherent* condition, it is the result of enormous legislative and fiscal burdens placed by Government on the business process which make marketing and customer satisfaction secondary to grant chasing, VAT collecting, tax manipulation and employment legislation. Such a regime gives a considerable advantage to the South East based lawyer, accountant or political lobbyist over the regional entrepreneur.

THE GENERAL EFFECTS OF REGIONAL POLICY

Perhaps the most important omission in the pursuit of Regional Policy has been the failure even to define the relative economic

47

position of the regions of the United Kingdom. There is no comprehensive collection of data on regional balance of payments. How can Government therefore even define the problem, never mind monitor the progress of its solutions? Balance of Payments for all the Regions of the UK must be prepared on an annual basis. These would include all *fiscal* flows and a "balance sheet" of ownership of regional equity.

The present system of financial support for the development areas in the United Kingdom is an unwieldly mechanism for encouraging wealth and job creation in the Regions. Indeed the system has concentrated support on those characteristics (capital goods in heavy industry or *employment* subisidies of up to £37,000 per job) which are often totally irrelevant to the promotion of value added – the very basis of long term industrial success and *real* job creation.

Henderson's study of company openings and closures showed that mobile manufacturing plants (the type which Government Regional Grants have subsidised into the. poorer Regions for many decades) have the worst closure record (TABLE 3). Although much of the bias towards manufacturing has been removed from the present regional aid system, there is no reason to assume that promoting *employment* through Government subsidy is going to be any more successful. There will merely be a new set of economic distortions, with queues of businessmen seeking subsidy for marginal industrial investments and taking advantage of funds raised predominantly from the Region in question.

Table 3
Scottish Manufacturing Plant Closures
R. A. Henderson Scottish Journal of Political Economy June 1980
Closure Ratios for each type of opening and destination 1966-1975
(openings within the period which closed within the period)

Destination	Inter-regional moves (including moves from abroad)		
	1966-71	1972-75	1966-75
Scotland	132	159	135
Peripheral Areas	106	144	114
Rest of UK	89	45	79
Total UK	100	100	100
	Intra-regional moves		
Scotland	112	94	108
Peripheral Areas	95	114	95
Rest of UK	102	92	102
Total UK	100	100	100

Enterprises new to manufacturing			
Scotland	149	151	144
Peripheral Areas	115	151	114
Rest of UK	93	68	93
Total UK	100	100	100
All new openings			
Scotland	127	136	125
Peripheral Areas	107	144	110
Rest of UK	96	70	94
Total UK	100	100	100

Peripheral areas: Scotland, Wales, Northern Ireland, North, North West, South West.

One of the principal problems in attracting *mobile factories* with subsidies rather than reducing taxes on *indigenous industry* is that factories have a considerably shorter life (usually product or market life) than does a company. Typically factories become obsolete (even in successful companies) within 10 – 20 years. Townsend writes: "It seems plausible that many of the intitial regional policy factories set up in the 1960's and before were reaching obsolescence together when the onset of severe recession precipitated closure."

As can be seen from TABLE 2 the subsidies to employment have succeeded in reducing the *variation* in regional unemployment rates although absolute levels have increased. In other words, despite the injection of many billions of pounds in regional aid, the very aspect of economic life which creates employment – wealth – has increased relatively in the prosperous areas and relatively decreased in the poorer areas.

The preservation of outdated industrial assets merely to massage regional unemployment has been one of the principal ingredients in overall economic (and hence employment) decline. The cost of (relatively less) unemployment for the regions was much greater (absolute) unemployment for everyone!

This approach is expressed in a recent policy statement:

"The modernisation projects will receive grant only if and to the extent that they create jobs". (Department of Trade & Industry).

Jobs are not at all the same thing as wealth creation – although wealth creation will in the long run create jobs – and capital investment tends not to increase employment. Over the last 15 years 56% of regional investment grants have gone to just four sectors – coal and petroleum, chemicals, metal manufacture and

49

food, drink and tobacco. All have suffered serious loss of employment although, with the exception of metal manufacturing, they have increased profitability (TABLE 4).

Table 4

REGIONAL DEVELOPMENT GRANTS

Manufacturing or Services?

56% of Grants between 1972 and 1984 went to 4 manufacturing sectors:

Coal and Petroleum products	9%	All large
Food Drink Tobacco	10%	job losers.
Chemical and Allied Ind	23%	
Metal manufacture	14%	

Sectors which did not qualify:

Finance	
Retailing	All large
Advertising	job gainers
Consultancy	

United Kingdom distribution of employment

	Agriculture	Manufacture	Services
1940	5%	40%	19%
1980	1.5%	31%	60%

On the other hand real employment growth has occurred in sectors – food distribution and retailing or finance – which never qualified for Government grants, even though the natural tendency of all healthy advanced industrial economies is to progress towards levels of services employment of about 70%. This preoccupation with manufacturing is even more incomprehensible when statistics show how valuable service employment is to the Regions of Britain which have exhibited the highest growth. (TABLE 5).

Table 5

RICHEST AND POOREST UK REGIONS

% OF EMPLOYEES IN SERVICES

3 Richest Regions: (1984)	% Employees in Service Sector (1)
South East	63.1
South West	59.0
East Anglia	56.8
4 Poorest Regions	
Wales	52.9
Yorks/Humberside	51.8
North	51.5
West Midlands	47.3

(1) After subtracting those employed in public administration

As office employment opportunities grew strongly in the South, Government grants attracted increasing numbers of manufacturing establishments to the peripheral areas. Much of this inward investment was foreign owned so that even when such investment could rival the value added of the service sector, the capital appreciation involved benefited external equity holders.

It is perhaps not surprising that the richest part of the United Kingdom – the South East suffered the greatest *outflow* of manufacturing establishments between 1945 and 1981 while the three poorest areas (excluding Northern Ireland) enjoyed high net inflows of such investment:

Table 6

The movement of manufacturing establishments

1945 – 1981

Region	Outflow	Inflow	Net Moves
South East	1842	195	−1647
North	55	420	+365
Wales	40	626	+586
Scotland	64	367	+303

Source: Armstrong and Taylor
"Regional Policy: The way forward"
Employment Institute

Grant aid and tax allowances give a subsidy to those who move *into* a region to the detriment of established companies – particular examples have been noted in the Enterprize Zones. The "front end" nature of subsidies and the lack of local equity encourages marginal and hence risky investment in (usually cheap) indigenous labour by remote corporations. The downside risk is minimal, the upside potential to foreign shareholders considerable.

A survey of American companies located in the North East of England found that on average only 34% of their supplies were sourced in the region – and it is probable that they were the least sophisticated of supplies.

Peterlee, the new town in Co. Durham (founded 1948) presents a suitable case study in the effects of attracting the mobile branch plants of (mostly foreign) coporations. 50% of the top 8 employers in 1986 were overseas companies and the *nearest* of the eight had its headquarters 120 miles away from Peterlee. Between 1955 and 1983 60 of the 143 companies

51

attracted to Peterlee had closed. This may not be a high percentage for start up companies but most were long standing companies merely *extending* operations to Peterlee. Even in 1985/86 when 1022 new jobs were created 526 jobs were lost. This high turnover of companies and jobs is a natural consequence of the *artificial* boost to incoming companies by Government grants and subsidies.

Even if grants were to benefit only British companies, do State subsidies lead to rational investment and hence long term corporate health and job creation? A questionnaire carried out by the Department of Trade and Industry in 1976 reveals how the priortities of companies change when confronted by Government incentives. The respondents were asked to list the most important factors influencing the decisions to locate operations in a particular area. The first three critiera were hardly the most commercially rational for stable investments!

Typical factors for investment decisions	1976 DTI questionnaire on factors influencing location
Return on Assets	Labour Availability
Market	Regional incentives
Labour availability	Local Authority Aid

If the Government is – at last– worried about grants being used to shift employment from one region to another it seems less worried about foreign companies doing the same on a global scale and using the subsidy to undermine British competitors. (As American fork lift truck manufacturer Hyster moved to Scotland with a £20m subsidy, the British fork lift truck manufacturer Lansing Bagnall made 250 redundant).

An American company Damon Biotech was supported by the British Government and the Scottish Development Agency to open a large factory in Livingstone, Scotland to produce a new product for which the research and development had still not been completed. Of the $40m cost of the project was to provide only $3m. Although the factory has been constructed there is considerable doubt about the commercial viability of the project. The British taxpayer should be concerned not only about the financial cost of this venture but should share the concern of the chief executive of the major British company in the biotechnology field, Celtech, who had every reason to object to this very large subsidy for a foreign competitor.

Even under the recently amended legislation grants are payable both to expand existing capacity and to create new production *regardless of whether there is already over-capacity in UK or world markets.* This is the kind of non-commercial activity which only Government is repeatedly capable of instigating. Market production capacities must be taken into account before making regional development grants, even if this requires intensive market research and co-ordination with other countries.

Much of those funds available for regional developments, especially those from European sources such as the European Coal and Steel grants, are only available through official institutions (an often intimidating bureaucratic barrier except to those large corporations who hardly require subsidy anyway) and are so narrowly defined as to exclude many commercially viable prospects.

For instance, in areas where there has been a decline in steel, coal or textiles, small new businesses in those sectors are not eligible for funds to finance market research and feasibility studies. Help is also often available to "service" industries so restrictively defined as to exclude those high value added and exportable services which would most benefit the regional balance of payments. In other words a local laundry or window cleaner servicing manufacturing industry would qualify for such support but a financial service or business consultancy with international customers (earning to the benefit of both regional and national balance of payments) will often not qualify.

Table 7 **DESTINATION OF JOBS MOVED FROM CENTRAL LONDON BY LOCATION OF OFFICES BUREAU CLIENTS; 1963-1979**

Region	Number of Moves	%	Number of Jobs	%
South East	1,808	81	116,762	73
of which:				
Greater London	808	37	51,544	32
Outer Metropolitan	734	33	44,017	27
Outer South East	260	12	21,201	13
East Anglia	54	2	5,606	4
South West	107	5	15,289	10
West Midlands	46	2	2,147	1
East Midlands	57	3	5,167	3
Yorkshire and Humberside	30	1	6,059	4
North West	58	3	5,268	3
North	21	1	2,254	1
Wales	16	1	449	–
Scotland	22	1	624	–
Northern Ireland	3	–	25	–
Total	2,222	100	160,100	100

Source: Location of Offices Bureau Statistical Handbook

53

Not only do Government regional grants often inhibit growth where a stimulus is intended but incentives tend to support regions which need no support – as when the Relocation of Offices Bureau caused 83% of corporate moves and 73% of job moves to go from London to other locations in the South East rather than to the depressed regions.

Business relocation in the pursuit of regional development grants caused so many jobs to move from the relatively prosperous West Midlands that it was eventually designated a development area itself. TABLE 8 shows also how the general fiscal balance moved betweeen the centre and the West Midlands during the 1970's so that despite the decline of its manufacturing base the Region was contributing more (as a percentage of its receipts) to the Exchequer than the prosperous South East.

Table 8

BALANCE OF GOVERNMENT/REGIONAL TRANSFERS 1974-1978
AND
CHANGE ON REGIONAL GDP PER HEAD 1971-1984

Region	Tax on Regions as % of Expenditure (1)	Change in GDP Per Head 71-84 (2)
North	94	+4
Yorkshire/Humberside	109	−6
East Midlands	108	+2
East Anglia	109	+4
South East	112	+4
South West	89	+1
Wales	92	−2
West Midlands	120	−12
North West	103	+1
Scotland	90	+4

Between 1971 and 1984 the West Midlands went from second richest to third poorest Region.

Source: (1) Derived from John Short "Public Finance and Devolution" Journal of Political economy June 1980.
(2) Regional Trends.

This table, unlike the misleading academic and political debate on *overt* "Regional Policy", demonstrates the true economic and fiscal relationship between the Centre and the poorer Regions and it is an extraordinary indictment of State intervention in this field.

The statistics compiled by Short in the 1970's are not easily reproduced for the 1980's – not least because much of the data required are no longer collected by Government. However the picture of the North – one of the poorest regions in the country – contributing 94% of its own "aid" is now almost certainly worse since (ostensible) regional aid has been reduced and general taxation has become more regressive thus taxing the poorer regions more (in relation to income) than the richer regions. Even on the basis of the 1970's statistics it would mean that of the circa £130m granted to Nissan to move to Sunderland some £120m was probably contributed by the very Region which central Government claims to be "aiding".

Regional Development Grants continue to benefit non-indigenous companies (at the expense of indigenous companies) long after they have been attracted to the poorer Regions. In the North East recent statistics show that by far the greatest share of the RDG's go to companies outside the Region. The DTI list of grants awarded in the 3rd quarter on the 1986/87 fiscal year show that 83% of grants went to non-indigenous companies.

Regional Development Grants 3rd Quarter 1986/87

North East of England

Total grant	£12.7m	
of which indigenous cos	£2.14m	(17%)
of which non-indigenous cos	10.56m	(83%)

Source: DTI Newcastle and own calculations

Since 80% of employment in North East *manufacturing* is now (after many decades of such grants!) owned by companies headquartered outside the Region these figures may not seem surprising, not least since the State's subsidies emphasised *mobile capital intensive* investment.

However recent changes in development grants cover a greater percentage of the UK workforce, reduce capital grants, put a limit on grant subsidy per job and withdraw grants for *replacement* plant and machinery. This latter measure is a further source of bias against long standing indigenous regional industry and in favour of external and foreign companies moving into a region. Nevertheless in general these changes seem to be having the effect of directing more grants towards indigenous companies than was the case under the old scheme.

Old Scheme grants:	Total	10.53m	
	Of which		
	Indegenous cos	1.22m	(12%)
	"Foreign" cos	9.31m	(88%)
New Scheme:	Total	£2.23m	
	Of which		
	Indigenous cos	0.93m	(44%)
	"Foreign" cos	1.30m	(56%)

However even this (perhaps temporarily) improved picture cannot mitigate the basic criticism that central Government continues to tax a Region's own resources in order to provide that Regions aid – with all the wasteful concomitant bureaucracy at both ends of this process.

What evidence is there of any mitigating advantage to the poorer Regions from 50 years of regional aid from the Centre? Townroe writes:

> "During the 1960's and 1970's small towns and rural areas were gaining both jobs and population, the gain in manufacturing jobs in relative terms being particulary sharp. *This pattern was exhibited in Assisted Areas and non Assisted Areas alike.*" (my emphasis).

If the characteristics of mobile manufacturing jobs which Government sought to promote were prominent in areas which Government aid did *not* cover then why subsidise *other* areas? The characteristics of the areas *naturally* favoured by investors cannot in real terms be reproduced in other areas merely through Government financial subsidy. Indeed subsidies attached to a *location* help to retain the very outmoded low value added industrial assets which accelerate that region's decline.

And what of Government relocation of jobs under its own control? There has been a deliberate policy by Governments of all political hues to locate Government administrative staff in the Regions (TV and car licences in Wales, DHSS in Newcastle, Manpower Services Commission in Sheffield) while the regional offices of the various Ministries have not been slow to recruit higher level managerial, technical and research staff. These moves – despite Union opposition – have not been very unpopular with civil servants and Government – a good reason for voters and consumers to be suspicious! Centrally determined

56

civil service salaries my be inadequate for London but they can be very attractive in Wales or Yorkshire. Such moves:

(a) distort rewards in the local labour market

(b) add no self generating wealth to the Region concerned

(c) bypass the need for basic salary differentials within the public sector.

Not only is there little evidence of the success of regional policies there is every sign that in areas badly in need of industrial investment Government aid has been spent on property, higher wages and luxury goods. After more than 20 years of the highest levels of regional aid the North, although continuing to lose jobs and companies, exhibited an extraordinary high life style. The average household in the North spends 50% more of its income on tobacco and alcohol than the South East and possesses more video recorders than any other part of the country except the South East.

(*Source*: Regional Trends 1986).

1980 Percentage of Households possessing

	North	South East
Central heating	61%	59%
Washing machine	85%	67%
Colour television	70%	67%

(*Source*: Regional Trends)

These 1980 statistics are of particular importance since they describe a situation at the end of a decade which saw the largest regional subsidies ever given by central Government. Even in 1984/85 (the most recent statistics) the North's consumer patterns compare favourably with the richest region in the South East:

1984/5 Percentage of Households possessing

	North	South East
Washing machine	85%	75%
Colour television	85%	85%

(*Source*: Regional Trends)

Although the North's unemployment level is twice that of the South East personal disposable income is only 20% less. Between 1969 and 1984 the top three regions for growth in average incomes were Northern Ireland, Greater London and Northern England. The poorer regions of the United Kingdom may be poor in terms of investment, wealth creation and employment but not in terms of wages, spending and luxury goods. Such an apparently unsustainable position has been preserved through the intervention of central Government. It could only be sustained on the basis of a misconception about the real value of regional industry and those who work in them and at the cost of long term industrial growth.

The most important ingredient in the success of a regional economy is its ability to retain, motivate and reward its most able school leavers and graduates. For the poorer regions of the United Kingdom the opposite has been the case. Former pupils of public and private sector schools of high academic achievement in Newcastle, Glasgow and Manchester are now to be found in central Government service, in southern Universities and in the London headquarters of the major corporations.

Productive and creative employment opportunities arise out of the production of goods and services valuable to customers. Those employed in industry and commerce respond to the stimulus of social and economic *change* and the awareness of an openness to such change comes from a competitive market and rational shareholders seeking the optimum use of physical and human resources. Where central Government has injected resources into a declining region it has done so through State industries and agencies and local authorities – none of which are open to commercial stimulus or disciplines. The most able are therefore driven to find creative and commercial outlets outside the very Region which most requires their ability. They migrate, marry and raise their children elsewhere, thus severing the geographic, cultural and family connection with their Region of origin.

Although this general process is inevitable to a certain extent in all societies, the drain of human resources from Regions to the centre in the UK is unparalleled in other western countries. But where central Government fiscal, monetary and legislative activity drains the Regions of their capital then human resources will inevitably follow. This process is perhaps even more serious than the Regional Equity Loss which is discussed in the next chapter.

REGIONAL EQUITY LOSS

A recent submission by an academic research group to the Secretary of State for Trade and Industry praises regional policy for attracting overseas investment into the Northern Region and simultaneously points out that considerable instability arises from the Region's high vulnerability to control outside the region.

Perhaps the most critical aspect of Government intervention in the economies of the Regions of the United Kingdom is what I term "Regional Equity Loss". All grants and subsidies to externally owned and foreign corporations financed by taxation of those individuals and corporations indigenous to a region involve equity loss. Capital owned in the region is recycled into support for projects and companies owned by external shareholders. These often very large grants, tax allowances or subsidised loans involve no sacrfiice of equity by those external owners of capital who benefit – even though such "front end" funds bear all the risks of venture capital for British taxpayers. In addition, by awarding tax allowances to corporations which pay most of their taxes outside the UK, indigenous companies – even those which have claimed similar reliefs in the development areas – have to pay almost all their taxes under a regime from which their foreign competitors are given relief.

The combination of taxes on the poorer regions, the redistribution through local Government and State agencies (employing well educated local labour which would otherwise be attracted into industry) and the subsidies to foreign and non-indigenous shareholders to establish peripheral "branch plants" (with most supplies coming from outside the Region or from firms owned outside the Region) has contributed to long term patterns of ownership, employment and cash flow which are damaging to the poorer Regions and extremely difficult to reverse.

Once a young graduate in Newcastle, Manchester or Glasgow has been recruited into local Government or the local office of the Department of Employment or Environment (with a salary generous by local labour market conditions) and is established in safe employment with secured pension rights he is unlikely to move to industrial employment either in that Region or anywhere else.

Once an indigenous entrepreneur or company has been taxed and his taxes used to finance externally owned regional assets and jobs then there is established a permanent outward flow of value added and dividends cancelling any positive effect of exports achieved by indigenous companies (or Government transfers).

A more obvious loss of corporate control and equity to a

59

Region is through takeover. Although it is always the quoted company takeover which excites regional headlines (among recent examples were Pilkington, Royal Bank of Scotland, Westland, Hillards) it is in fact the takeover of the smaller private company (usually entirely locally owned) which involved the biggest loss of regional equity. The larger corporations, quoted on the Stock Exchange, usually have a very wide shareholding unrelated to the Region in which they operate although local loyalties can be significant). However, even the takeover of such companies does involve a loss of regional managerial control and, as Dennis Henry has demonstrated many serious knock on effects in ancillary services which add value to the regional economy (accounting, legal).

An important factor in regional industrial weakness is the effect of mergers, acquisitions and disposals of firms outside the Regions which have subsidiaries within the Region. *With such changes of ownership it is as probable that companies will be closed for internal structural reasons as for reasons of profitability.* Healthy local corporations are acquired either to frustrate competition or to aquire technological innovation. Because of the dominance of the London capital markets and central Government taxation policies the Regional economy has no capital resources to outbid external predators. Acquired companies are often closed (to reduce supply in the market) or become branch plants with no R & D facility, no senior management but with mass production on a decreasing number of product lines. These are classic ingredients for business vulnerability.

TABLE 9 shows the effect of takeovers of smaller companies in the North East of England over recent years. Although this is not a full list of such takeovers the trends are disturbing from a regional industrial view.

Table 9

THE RESULTS OF COMPANY TAKEOVERS IN THE NORTH EAST

Company	Acquired by + date	Job loss/closure
Fidus Controls Est 1978. Big demand for product, low capital base	Agreed takeover by BUNZL 1978	Closed and production Transferred 1981 to Bletchley.
Hughes (Blyth) Ltd Est 1974	Rapid growth, sold out to Danish firm VTM 1979	Closed 1981.
Tyne Chemicals only UK producer of cathode foil	Taken over 1969 by USA company Wellington Technical Industries. Despite world shortage production run down	Closed 1976.
Roconeco. Est 1981 a joint venture UK & US companies. Only UK manufacturer of road planing machines	Sold to Ingersoll Rand 1982	Closed 1985.
S. Maclean & Co Ventilators	Acquired by Novenco 1972 then by Danish company Danske Sukkerfabriker 1982	Immediately closed and production moved to Sheffield.
Joplings Steel	Acquired by Wm Clark of Sheffield	Immediately closed. 1986 250 jobs lost.
Northumberland Press	Parent company Richard Clay taken over by St Ives Group, London	Closed 1986. 50 jobs lost.
Camrex Paints	Parent Camrex plc taken over by Ruberoid, 1983	Closed 1986. 200 jobs lost.
Union Carbide	Acquired by STC 1981	Closed 1982. 500 jobs lost.
McGregor Wallcovering	Acquired by Berger Paints	Closed 1980. 100 jobs lost.
Head Wrightson Steelcast	Taken over by Davy in 1976	Closed in 1978. 120 jobs lost.
GEC Elliott Processing	Taken over by Fischer Controls in 1979	Closed in 1979. 250 jobs lost.

Some were the subsidiaries of externally owned companies prior to further takeover; some were in decline and takeover could be regarded as a rescue (initially at least); some were the manufacturers of unique or unusual products, the acquisition of which was more important than the company itself; some were successful and growing so rapidly as to welcome takeover as a source of extra capital. What ever the reason these various needs could have been accommodated equally well if local companies and investors had been in a position to acquire or inject capital into these companies.

TABLE 10 shows how the North East has lost control of many of its quoted companies over recent years. Between 1971 and 1984 the North East lost control of 9 of its 14 companies in the Times top 1000.

Table 10

UK Rank*	INDEPENDENTS IN 1971	ACQUIRING COMPANY	YEAR OF TAKEOVER	INDEPENDENTS IN 1984 (RANK)
130	Swan Hunter Group	British Shipbuilders/ Ferguson Ind. Holdings		
131	Reyrolle Parsons	NEI)		103
280	Whessoe			450
345	Clarke Chapman	NEI		
384	Wrights Biscuits	Cavenham/United Biscuits	72	
399	Vaux breweries			460
449	Head Wrightsons	Davy International	76	
491	Steel Group	Acrow/Groves Cranes	72	
504	Doxford & Sunderland Group	Court Line/ British Shipbuilders	72	
542	Hawthorn Leslie	Starwest Holdings	81	
558	K Shoe	C & J Clark	81	
587	Richardson Westgarth			745
596	J. W. Cameron	Ellerman Lines	75	
767	Camrex Holdings	Ruberoid	83	
918	Hugh McKay	(Allied Textiles)**	(85)	
988	Crossley Building Products	Bowater Corporation	78	

*Rank by turnover   **Minority holding

Source: Ian Smith Northern Economic Review Winter 1985/86

As with the smaller companies it is largely a question of regional capital retention rather than takeover policy or prevention. When regional individual savings are diverted to centralised institutional investors through Government fiscal manipulation than to speak of a free market in capital and equal opportunities for regional companies and investors is grossly misleading. It is to these fiscal distortions that we turn in the next chapter.

One of the most disturbing aspects of Government intervention in the economy is the almost total lack of adequate data and research on which even a preliminary analysis could be based, never mind a comprehensive programme. This is true of the field of regional corporate takeovers. Dennis Henry has exposed as dangerously misleading a recent study of takeovers in Scotland which – with statistics up to 1980! – declared that takeovers were not detrimental to the Scottish economy. Henry's own statistics on takeovers of quoted industrial and commercial companies shows how much the picture has changed since 1980.

Takeovers of quoted Industrial/Commercial in Scotland

Years	Number per annum	Employment in those companies in year of takeover (Average)
1965-80	3.3	31,722
1985-86	7	94,960

The more immediate direct consequencies for a regional economy of a corporate takeover are usually all too obvious to company, workforce and Government policy makers. However the local knock-on effects are less obvious, indirect and delayed but of no less significance.

Takeovers of Scottish Companies – Impact on Local Services

Net Change

Materials	−24%
SERVICES	−72%
of which:	
Auditors	−52
Banks	−40
Lawyers	−24
Others	−16

Source: Industry Department for Scotland. Quoted by Henry.

Such professional occupations as banking, accountancy and the law probably add considerably more value to the local economy than managerial personel within the corporation which has been taken over.

The Regional Development Agencies

It has long been a complaint of the English Regions that Wales and Scotland have been relatively more successful in attracting new investment. This is ascribed to the two regional "umbrella organisations" (the Welsh and Scottish Development Agencies) which have acted as a focal point for information and support for potential investors. They have been able to "speak as one voice" not only to domestic investors and foreign companies but also to central Government. However, others have ascribed Scottish and Welsh success to their national and cultural identities and specific Ministerial responsibility in London.

The recently established Northern Development Company, intended to represent the interests of the North arose partly out of the success of the Region in attracting the Nissan car factory to Washington, Co. Durham. However, there is already a plethora of organisations in the Northern Region researching, analysing, promoting and providing grants, subsidies and advice to businessmen. The NDC has an important role to play but its success will depend on a considerable pruning and rationalisation of existing – and to a large extent competing sensitivity to the consequences of macro economic policy pursued in London.

However, this paper is concerned not so much with the form of such Regional organisations but with their activities and the way those activities are dictated by central Government policy towards the Regions.

For if Scotland's recent success is largely due to North Sea Oil (where most of the value added is siphoned off to the UK Exchequer and American oil and oil supply companies): and if Wales and Scotland have merely been short term beneficiaries of Japanese and American electronics companies seeking subsidies and low cost labour (50% of Scotland's electronics companies are American or Japanese owned) then the Welsh and Scottish Development Agencies will have done little more than make their regions more dependent on foreign shareholders and London institutions. If the above analysis is well founded than this is not the model which the new Northern Development company, or any other Region, should be encouraged to follow.

FISCAL DISTORTIONS OF REGIONAL ECONOMIES

The most important elements in the analysis of regional wealth should therefore be the National Tax regime, individual patterns of savings and investment, the regional balance of equity ownership and the characteristics of entrepreneurs. Political notions of regional "assistance" have unfortunately taken a different approach.

For many years inflation represented the depletion of money savings, like Bank and Building Society deposits (predominantly held by the less well off in the Regions) and a boost to non monetary assets, like houses and land (predominantly the South). Inflation is also a transfer to central Government – through the devaluing of its debt – while Clearing Banks, (based in the South) were the main beneficiaries of the inflationary process itself.

Capital Taxation in the UK – even after recent changes – cuts in at very low levels of "wealth" and what reliefs there are tend to favour institutional investment, forestry and farms rather than family businesses and personal investment. "Wealth" taxes like

64

Inheritance Tax are not dissimilar to inflation in their effect – funds are diverted from personal investors to institutional lenders and from the regions to the centre.

High taxes in general reduce the market power of individuals and increase the scope for political decisions in London. Even if monies are channelled back through tax allowances the form those allowances take is determined by London based interest groups, strategically close to Whitehall and Westminster. Indeed, so detrimental are some of the effects of Government re-injection of funds into the Regions that, paradoxically, it might be better if such re-injection did not occur! Government grants and subsidies raise the price of many vital local resources out of the reach of *local* businesses and attract many educated and skilled *potential* businessmen into the mere administration of grants. If no such re-injection took place then at least the remaining non financial resources would reach the price level at which regional companies and entrepreneurs could afford to take risks.

In order to counteract fiscal privileges for Pension Fund investment the Government introduced an equivalent subsidy for tax payers to invest directly in small companies – the Business Expansion Scheme. Here again it is high tax payers (mainly in the South) who receive the subsidy and the BES *funds* which are predominantly based and managed in the City of London where they are unlikely to detect good investment opportunities in the Regions.

In the Northern Region, where there is a need for business creation and expansion there is no regionally based Business Expansion Scheme. BES funds give *individuals* tax relief, not financial institutions so that any BES fund manager must base his earnings on commissions on each investment made (not just on money raised). Such schemes are therefore *turnover* not investment dependent. A similar situation exists in the public sector where various local initiatives (enterprise agencies, technology centres, science parks etc) find they must go outside their locality to raise activity to a level which justifies their agency (see work by Segal Quince & Wicksteed).

These local institutions which wish to establish a regional BES scheme, cannot justify the time required to negotiate such a scheme with the Inland Revenue, set up the separate bureaucratic system required and monitor and report on the investments made since the turnover of potential BES deals in the Region could not compensate for such a workload.

If there is a place for a Business Expansion Scheme if should be for direct investment in the regions (by regional investors) *only*, rather than for high marginal tax payers based in prosperous regions. But it would be preferable to remove the fiscal bias towards institutional savings in general so that the counter balancing distortion of BES would not be necessary.

The virtual monopoly of Stock Exchange and merchant banking activities in London (aided by lucrative Government contracts and a regular throughput of Government debt instruments) and the fiscal privileges of London based or managed pension funds leave both regional investors and companies at a disadvantage.

Mortgage interest relief is a Government intervention which gives most to those who are wealthiest (in the South) and least to those who are poorest (in the North). In addition it has seduced many into unsustainable house ownership in depressed areas where their properties are unsaleable.

The house price distortions promoted by mortage interest relief also deter senior management and skilled workers in the South (often emigre Northerners) from moving North where they are most needed since they risk the prospect of never being able to re-enter the South's higher priced housing market. The whole edifice of tax allowances surrounding the ownership of a house encourages deposits in Building Societies which are predominantly based in the wealthier South and tends to divert what investible funds there are in poorer regions into house purchase. Between 1972 and 1982 houses prices rose by 285% in the North – far faster than in London (142%) even though employment over a similar period fell by twice as much (North – 14%, South East – 7%).

It has been noted that even high unemployment in a region does not deflect from the artificial incentive provided by Government for house speculation.

> "Borrowers in relatively depressed areas are taking on larger mortgage commitments both relative to income and relative to house prices than they did six years ago."
> Lloyds Bank Economic Bulletin September 1986

74% of the Building Societies which benefit from this kind of fiscal distortion have headquarters south of a line from North

Wales to the Wash. The effect of Mortgage Interest Tax relief on the relative position of the poorer regions versus the South East can be seen from TABLE 11.

Table 11

HOUSE MORTGAGE SUBSIDY
REGIONAL DISTRIBUTION 1984

REGION	NUMBER OF LOANS	TOTAL ADVANCES	12% INTEREST	SUBSIDY AT 30% TAX RATE
North	53,000	873m	104m	31.2m
Yorkshire/Humberside	107,000	1738m	208m	62.4m
London/South East	337,000	8569m	1028m	308m

THE EFFECT OF HOUSE PRICES 1984

REGION	AVERAGE HOUSE PRICE	AVERAGE INCOME OF BORROWERS	HOUSE PRICES: INCOME
North	22,604	9,914	2.28
Yorkshire/Humberside	22,356	9,124	2.45
London/South East	38,340	12,968	2.96

Source: Building Societies Association (Own calculations)

When a tax relief is granted by Government to guide expenditure in directions which the *State* deems beneficial then it is the highest rate taxpayers who benefit most. Since most of this category live in the South East (eg the South East has 25% more people in the £10,000 plus bracket than the North) then it is not surprising that – even assuming a 30% tax rate – London and the South East receive £270m more from just this one tax expenditure that the North.

In a market like housing, when the period between perceived demand and completion of supply is both long and inflexible, demand – and in particular money demand – is the principal influence on prices. Indeed there is much evidence (see Atkinson 1986) that money demand is siphoned off by house builders and Building Societies rather than finding its way through into extra house production. The result of Government's fiscal largesse in the housing market is that the house price to income ratio in the South East is 2.96 against 2.28 in the North – at least partly a demonstration of the potency of higher marginal tax rates.

The other major tax expenditures which help to institutional-ise both funds and investment decisons in the South (Business Expansion Scheme and Pension Fund contributions) also benefit the higher rate tax payer. The latter costs the Exchequer £6.5 billion per annum (as against £4.5 billion for Mortgage Interest Relief) and the regional effects of this expenditure are likely to be at least as redistributive from the poorer regions. Indeed pension fund tax relief is so well established as a tax saving device that the highest marginal tax payers are more likely to predomionate than in, say, Mortgage Interest Relief where the prime aim is usually house purchase. The possible extent of tax expenditures' "taxation" of the poorer Regions can be gauged from the fact that in 1985/86 the Exchequer cost of such allowances was £18 billion.

Assuming a similar "skewed" distribution of the benefits of such allowances betweeen the North and the South East as in the Mortgage Interest Relief example, then the advantage to the South East could be £1,000m per annum – about twice the 1983/84 Government expenditure on Regional Development Grants and Selective Assistance for *all* areas.

Other central Government fiscal attempts to promote industrial and economic success have also exacerbated regional differences. The regional effects of the Government's loan guarantee scheme can be seen in TABLE 10. The Business Expansion Scheme relies on taxing everyone and then returning taxes to those who can do certain things in certain kinds of company at certain stages of development and who have administrative and geographic access to those institutions which run such schemes (nearly always dominated by London based Banks and investment funds).

Table 12

SMALL BUSINESS LOAN GUARANTEE SCHEME: REGIONAL DISTRIBUTION

Region	Number of Loans June 1981-June 1982	Number of Loans June 1981-Sept. 1983	Average value of a Loan, June 1981-Sept. 1983 £	Number of loans: Number of '000 businesses per region 1981-1982	Number of loans: Number of '000 businesses per region 1981-1983
North Eastern	182	534	30,150	3.7	10.9
North West	678	1666	30,972	4.9	12.1
Yorkshire & Humberside	381	962	28,898	3.5	8.9
West Midlands	488	1084	32,380	4.1	9.1
East Midlands	329	796	33,740	3.5	8.5
South East	1883	4569	36,157	4.0	9.8
South West	455	1117	31,781	3.3	8.0
Scotland	283	789	28,644	2.8	7.8
Wales	285	602	30,233	3.8	8.1
Northern Ireland	18	112	39,286	0.4	2.5

Total Loan amounts 1981-1983
South East £165m
North £16m

Source: Department of Trade and Industry

69

All Government schemes based on tax incentives for individuals will have a bias towards the South East – and the South East's tax payments reflect this over recent years. Average weekly earnings in the South East are 19% more than in the North but average income tax paid as a percentage of total income in the South East is only 16.5% more than in the North.

TABLE 13 compares the Northern Region with the South East on the basis of population, investment in non quoted companies (a recognised indicator of economic activity) and loans under the Loan Guarantee Scheme.

Table 13

Region	% UK Population	% of investment in non quoted cos	% loans under loan guarantees
North	25%	10%	4%
South East	30%	64%	43%

The table clearly demonstrates how Government *subsidies* for industry are channelled through institutions at the *centre* and exacerbate rather than relieve the differences between North and South. *Real* aid would come from Government withdrawal from fiscal manipulation, lower taxes in the Regions themselves and the promotion of individual savings and hence regional corporate investment.

It must be noted that the most significant distortion of Regional economies is not just in the tax expenditure and the raising of taxes (the abolition of the former should lead to lowering the latter) but in the institutional structures and price distortions which this direction of savings and investment brings about. It is the fact that Building Societies house builders, insurance companies, pension funds, large quoted corporations and investment managers benefit at the expense of house buyers individual investors, smaller unquoted companies and regional economies. Even after abolition of these allowances labour mobility will suffer for some time from house price differentials, individuals from corporate savings and regional economies from central institutions. But the sooner the tax system can be reformed the sooner a more rational and efficient process can begin.

THE REGIONS AND THE POLITICAL PROCESS

The enormous volume of legislation enacted in Westminster and in Europe has a vital impact on the economy of the Regions. There are many cases where legislaton or directives in Westminster or Brussels have caused Regional distortions which are then "balanced" by special allowances, subsidies and even more regional grants. There is no systematic monitoring of such leglislation by the Regions. The Department of Trade and Industry should either pay for the commercial monitoring of such legislation (by a Public Affairs Consultancy) or carry out such monitoring itself, providing monthly notice of all relevant forthcoming legislation.

When the various fiscal distortions and tax withdrawals from the Regions have been eliminated fewer funds will circulate through the Department of Trade and Industry and will instead remain within the Regions. The Department of Trade and Industry in London will therefore have sufficient time to carry out these moniotoring and reporting duties.

Regional Policy is conceived and conducted at the centre. It is primarily an activity influenced by politicians and lobbyists. If the regions are to influence events their political representatives must be of the highest calibre.

Regional policy is however researched and administered by civil servants who see the source of their career advancement in the South East. Regional Policy conceived as Government intervention is therefore influenced, financed and carried out by those who may have little or no direct interest in the Regions. A more effective policy in terms of long term wealth, employment prospects and regional independence can be achieved by a reduction in Government intervention, lower taxation of the regions in need and fewer fiscal distortions which draw capital and skills to the centre and increase the dependence of regional industry on external ownership.

Recent history indicates that the Regions have been badly served by central Government and a radical reappraisal of regional economic support is long overdue. The present structure of regional support (and taxation) should be rejected not least because it is based on a totally misleading analysis of the relationship between the centre and the Regions. The complete failure – over many decades – to recognise the Regional Equity Loss to the poorer regions should become a priority issue for politicians of all parties.

SUMMARY

1. Central Government Regional Policies have been in place for over 50 years but they have been an irrelevance since the true fiscal balance between the Centre and the Regions has been ignored. Even the poorest areas pay for 95% of their own aid.

2. The paper introduces the term REGIONAL EQUITY LOSS to describe the most debilitating process whereby local wealth creators are taxed and external investors subsidised, thereby establishing a long term drain of value added.

3. The principal beneficiaries of the policy have been mobile foreign corporations subsidised into competition with UK companies, taking a full equity stake while passing the commercial risk to the UK Government.

4. It is a disadvantage to British companies, taxed principally in the UK, if foreign companies are attracted to Britain with large reliefs from a tax regime to which they are not predominantly exposed. Tax reliefs from British taxes are financed by higher taxes on British companies and consumers.

5. The paper reviews the history and purpose of regional policy since the early 1930's and compares the levels and variations in regional unemployment in 1933 and 1986.

6. The definition and purpose of regional policy is examined in the light of 5 types of industrial change and their various time horizons (prices, products, factories, companies and industries).

7. The evidence for a "North South divide" is examined and "for all the exceptions and qualifications" this basic delineation is confirmed.

8. The paper analyses the distribution of Regional Development Grants between externally owned and indigenous companies in the northern region and shows how externally owned companies continue to receive the bulk of Government subsidy long after they have been attracted to the development areas.

9. The paper questions the extent of "local supplies" to externally owned companies in the North East and questions whether these are from local indigenous companies and to what extent they are "high value added" supplies.

10. Company openings and closures in Peterlee (a town which did not exist prior to 1948 and has been a major recipient of foreign inward investment) are analysed and the reason for employment instability sought.
11. Much empirical evidence of the effect of takeovers in the North East and Scotland is presented-in particular the effect on local services when major quoted companies are taken over.
12. The author identifies the failure to retain regional capital as the main cause of lack of regional corporate control and business expansion.
13. The migration of the most able graduates, skilled workers and entrepreneurs from the very regions which need them most is identified as a debilitating process for the poorer regions. This is an inevitable result when State funds are injected. The skilled, creative and enterprising are frustrated by a system closed to the stimulus of market service.

CONCLUSIONS

1. The author's research indicates that the immediate objective for regional policy should be to "raise GDP per head" in the poorer regions rather than "reduce unemployment for the existing population".
2. Central Government aid and subsidy have been financed by taxing the wealth creators within the very regions which require help. It would be beneficial therefore if taxes were reduced *within* the regions and tax allowances reduced *outside* thus helping to retain capital and human resources.
3. Similarly the new emphasis should be on regionally indigenous *companies* rather than externally owned *factories*, on economic pricing rather than Government subsidy and general profitability rather than certain kinds of investment which are thought to "create jobs".
4. "Tax expenditures" like mortgage interest relief, business expansions funds and relief for pension contributions not only disguise a large injection of funds into the richer regions (probably twice as much as the total amount spent on regional support) they establish centralised institutional control of capital and investment decisions rather than regional individual control. Gradual phasing out of these reliefs would aid regional development.

73

5. If the business expansion scheme is to be continued it would best be confined to development area investments *and investors* in the poorer regions.
6. The author's comparison between normal investment criteria for a successful company and those which the DTI found influenced development area investment indicates how Government subsidy can lead to poor investment decisions.
7. State owned industries (dominant in the poorer regions) were the biggest job losers in the mid 1970's and early 1980's. 18 of the 20 poorest towns in the UK either are or have been dominated by State owned steel, coal or shipbuilding.
8. Subsidised State industries, privatised monopolies and privatised industries ineffectively regulated can prevent rational regional investment decisions in energy, transport etc by their subsidised or monopoly activities. It is advocated that the Office of Fair Trading, OFTEL and OFGAS should be obliged to study the *regional* consequences of the operations of State and privatised industries.
9. Regional unemployment problems are not addressed by relocating central Government offices – indeed these moves are often distorting and counter productive since (a) they distort rewards in the local labour market (b) add no self generating wealth to the region concerned and (c) bypass the need for salary differentials within the public sector.
10. Regional pay differentials could be encouraged to reflect local labour costs. The Government could start with its own civil servants, doctors and State industry staff.
11. Government should monitor all industrial aid and small business promotion schemes to determine their regional effects.
12. There should be a general reduction in personnel administering grants in the regions with most support being automatic and fiscal. This would prevent the recruitment of a regions talent into public administration when local business is often critically short of management.
13. Although the principal cause of the loss of regional equity and companies is the fiscal drain of capital to the centre (see 4 above) the Monopolies and Mergers Commission must consider the Regional implications of merger and acquisition proposals. The Regions should also refer such proposals to the Commission. The regional offices of the

DTI should monitor smaller non quoted companies and encourage local financial institutions and investment funds to offer local capital to prevent takeover.

14. The abolition of Regional Development Grants for replacement plant and machinery is a bias against longer established indigenous companies on favour of new (and usually non-indigenous) companies.

15. Before regional grants and tax incentives are awarded to overseas companies a more rigorous survey of industrial capacity should be undertaken. Where there is excess capacity and/or significant (but not monopoly) UK corporate involvement, grants should not be awarded.

BIBLIOGRAPHY

H. Armstrong, J. Taylor	"Regional Policy – Dead or Alive?" The Economic Review November 1966.
A. G. Champion, A. E. Green	"In Search of Britain's Booming Towns".
Department of Trade & Industry	"Regional Industrial Policy – Some Economic Issues" London DTI 1983.
R. A. Henderson	"An analysis of closures amongst Scottish manufacturing plants betweeen 1966 and 1975" Scottish Journal of Political Economy 1980.
I. Smith	"Takeovers, Rationalisation and the Northern Region Economy" Northern Economic Review Nr 12.

J. Short

"Public Finance and Devolution: Money flows betweeen Government and Regions in the United Kingdom" Scottish Journal of Political Economy June 1984.

P. W. Townroe

"Regional Economic Development Policy in a mixed economy and a Welfare State".

A. R. Townsend, F. W. Peck

"The Geography of Mass Redundancy in named corporations."

D. Henry

"The Effect of Takeovers on the Scottish Economy" Unpublished contribution to a conference Regional Policy – A New Approach. Public Issue Conferences 1987.

R. E. B. Atkinson

"Government against the People" P.106-114 Compuprint Publishing 1986.

4 Corporate Takeovers and Regional Investment

Takeovers of important Northern companies have reached epidemic proportions.

Rowntree has been taken over, Scottish & Newcastle is threatened, NEI and Vaux have acquired unwelcome shareholdings from potential bidders. The North's leading stockbroker has lost its independence and the region's two leading estate agents have sold out to major financial institutions.

The brewer J W Cameron has suffered the fate of so many subsidiaries and branch factories typical of the North: its parent company has sold it to another company. The boards of two local water companies seem to prefer French cash to Northern independence.

Even the region's most successful investment institution, recently raising more funds for investment in Northern companies, finds that 90% of the new capital injected is from the South.

It is indeed ironic that, just as the North is beginning to recover from decades of industrial decline, our successful companies are being picked off before they can really contribute to regional wealth creation and, above all, *retention*.

It is altogether a sorry picture. No wonder that one of the region's most successful industrialists, Tom Cowie, would prefer to buy back his company from the stockmarket. The City of London looks increasingly like a casino for speculators in takeovers rather than a sophisticated source of capital for industry and a responsible market for investors.

The North and other "peripheral regions" of the UK are particularly vulnerable to takeovers as capital, human resources and investment power have been drained to the South-East. High income and capital taxes, nationalisation (and privatisation in equally centralised form), tax allowances which benefit London financial institutions and Government subsidies for quoted companies have all contributed to the concentration of financial and political power in the South.

Today the grandson of a Northern entrepreneur who built his wealth in the early part of this century is almost certainly in

London administering tax collection or managing an insurance company's share portfolio rather than trying to emulate his grandfather by setting up his own business in the North.

Where capital goes, people must follow. Few able Northerners have wished to stay in a region where Government grants for marginal "branch factories", politically inspired "infrastructure projects" or Government "job creation" represent the limit of business opportunities.

No Government since the 1930s can escape the blame for the malaise in the North, Scotland and Wales. London's "compassion" – financed by taxing those they claim to help – has led only to debilitating dependence on the State. And when the source of economic reward is the Government, then it is Southern politicians and businessmen who are best placed to benefit.

However, the traditional picture of Northern job losses, company closures and wealth destruction has, paradoxically, been accompanied by high consumer expenditure.

The North may have high unemployment, but we have the largest indoor leisure centre in Europe. We may be losing major companies but we still have Eldon Square shopping centre. We may have no significant financial institutions but we have the Metro Centre.

Give a poor man money and all you have is a poor man with money. Give a poor region Government grants and all you have is a poor region with money. Poor men and poor regions with money tend to *spend* it – on external companies, externally produced goods and therefore on generating jobs outside the region.

Wealth for a successful family, individual or region must be created by indigenous worth and skills. That wealth must be retained and invested in higher skills and better education, for only through such investment can wealth and jobs continue to grow. One generation does not make a family and a company which one man has established, his sons can expand. Selling out to the highest bidder today means that all the future value added will flow out of the family or region.

Those who had freedom and responsibility yesterday will be in unstable dependence on a remote owner tomorrow.

So can the North generate, retain, re-invest and control its own capital? Or will the average Northern family be forever dependent on London welfare, Brussels subsidy and Tokyo capital, employed to assemble microwave ovens this year, packing jelly babies next year and beating grouse for tourists the year after?

Will their most promising companies be taken over and closed as the technology which originated in the North profits a businessman in Surrey or California?

There is a real resurgence of home-based entrepreneurship in the North, but so often it is external capital to which the successful entrepreneur sells out. Too often growing companies see takeover by a company outside the region as a source of capital which is so sadly lacking locally.

Too often the first thought of the Northerner, be he successful businessman or well paid worker, is to spend rather than invest or buy property abroad rather than invest in local business. Too often the fate of our few major corporations is in the hands of London banks and investment institutions and Government while the North can only look on in impotence.

It is absloutely vital for the long term economic health of the North that businessmen, financial institutions, pension funds and (especially) individuals and families should have the opportunity of investing in their own future. A major Northern investment institution, funded by its own people, is badly needed, an institution which will put the skills and education of the workforce before property speculation, the North before London and business investment in their communities before financial investments in remote institutions.

It may we be that those who are considering these ideas for the North are whistling in the dark. Perhaps there is no interest in investing in our own companies, helping them to grow, create and retain wealth and maintaining their independence. But it would be a sad reflection on a region rightly regarded as one of the world's greatest industrial centres if its people were not prepared to invest in their own independence.

5 North – South and Scottish and Newcastle

Imagine two companies, A and B, competing in the same market. For many decades a third party with universal political and economic powers (let us call it "Government") had taken over or controlled many assets belonging to A, systematically reducing their value. Government responded to A's subsequent weakness by offering subsidies – but subsidies for only certain kinds of investment. Government thought that a certain kind of investment – manufacturing – was particularly worthy, even though B, without so many subsidies and controls was in fact prospering by divesting itself of manufacturing plant and increasing investment in service industries – for which A was explicitly denied any investment grant or subsidy.

Imagine further that A received many hundreds of millions of pounds from this Government over a period of 50 years, even though these grants were originally conceived as "transitional arrangements". Furthermore of every £1m given by Government A actually paid for at least £950,000 itself – in taxes. This circular process was in fact even worse than it might seem since it was the most profitable, experienced and enterprising parts of A which paid the taxes and the least profitable, least able and least industrious parts of A which received the subsidy. Indeed a very large percentage of the total flow of funds were even given to companies which were part of B and indeed to corporations overseas, often to A's and B's foreign competitors. This process was so widespread and long lasting that 80% of A's manufacturing assets were now controlled externally.

This extraordinary state of affairs often meant that A, which was regarded as so weak that it required "help" was in fact subsidising its competitors. A's capital was actually being diminished and the capital of rich and successful competitors enhanced.

Imagine also that after subsidising A's declining loss making assets well beyond their useful life many able entrepreneurs and skilled workers, anxious to *really* respond to consumers, were driven from A to B – where commercial business was on more rational and traditional lines. This is a natural reaction to State subsidy and control – those with any "get up and go" do just that. At this point the overall burden of taxation on both A and B was very high – subsidising ever greater areas of business is very costly. Therefore, instead of lowering taxes, tax *allowances* were extended – for mortgage interest relief, pension fund contributions, for pension and life assurance funds. This of course meant that no tax payer – and especially the higher rate tax payers in B (more able than those in A to afford sharp accountants) could afford *not* to invest in such ways. It was not surprising that B – geographically and institutionally much closer to Government – was able to lobby for and retain theses allowances which – low and behold – happened to concern those very commercial sectors – banking, pension funds, investment, life assurance – in which B specialised and which A was weak.

Even those most successful in A could not afford to ignore the tax allowances which directed their savings towards B. Rather than reinvest in A they "sheltered" their tax liability by taking out mortgages, life assurance and pension schemes run by B, thus further enhancing B's commercial, financial (and political) power.

After some time a new Government was elected and a new era of "market economics" began. State industries were privatised, taxes reduced and Government intervention (officially!) phased out. Suddenly Government refused to help A with so many subsidies – although it did nothing to reduce, *indeed in many areas it increased* the subsidies to financial investments in B.

So powerful was B in this new environment – both subsidised *and* liberated – that they were able to bid for and acquire (from their own investment institutions) those few assets of A which had managed to survive the decades long pummelling described above. Suddenly, having been drained of both capital and human resources for so long, A was now required to compete on equal terms with B which had been the principal beneficiary of A's demise. No race starts with the starters gun and those who believe they have created an environment of "market forces" overnight do more harm than those who would have retained debilitating controls.

It will by now be evident to readers of this sorry tale that A represents the Northern Regions of the United Kingdom, Scotland and Wales, often called the "peripheral" regions while B represents London and the South East. The event which prompts this analysis is the bid by Elders for Scottish and

Newcastle Breweries, the outcome of which will be influenced by London based banks who finance the bid, London based institutional investors who will vote the majority of the shares, and London based central Government which draws up the terms of reference for the Monopolies Mergers Commission Inquiry.

Should the bid succeed even a modest 10% rationalisation of Scottish and Newcastle's business would involve the loss of 2500 jobs – most of them in the North East of England, the poorest UK Region bar Nothern Ireland. The loss would be the equivalent to those jobs created after 10 years work and £150m in grants to attract the Nissan car factory to the same region.

It is time for Government to recognise the history of central control and subsidies which have distorted the commercial relations between North and South since the 1930's. The Government's reduction in income and capital taxes, the desire – by the Treasury at least – to reduce tax allowances and the recent strategy of privatising electricity and water industries along *regional* lines will help to build up and retain regional wealth and economic independence in the long run. In the interim it would be no contradiction of market economics to give major regional corporations a measure of protection. I am confident that, unlike regional development grants, *this* interim measure would not need to last 50 years.

PART THREE

The State

1 The Exploited Class

The Self-Employed and the State

Socialists believe that politicians and the State have the knowledge, compassion and ability to promote economic justice. Market capitalists believe that State controls cause more injustice than a system based on individual freedom and responsibility.

As the collectivist State – under all political parties – has increased its domination over post war Britain, inequalities have grown, not diminished. The arbitrary dispensing of State patronage to the politically acceptable and the pernicious of the commercially responsible have led to gross inequalities in the treatment of individuals of the same skills, education and enthusiasm.

If the skills of a worker in a State industry with a closed shop union become redundant he will receive a large payment, a pension related to final salary and help to find new employment. If on the other hand the skills of the self employed become redundant there often ensues bankruptcy, loss of savings, the loss of family home, and no State aid or redundancy payments. Such is the "equality" for which the State legislates.

Let us consider the fate of three shopkeepers in the North of England. Like so many of the enterprising self employed at the lower end of the earnings scale the cost and bureaucracy of becoming limited liability companies were rejected. Such businesses (unlike the middle class professions) require the financing of stock but debt for a sole trader is a serious personal (and family) liability. Mr S. was a teacher for many years before taking over the running of two shops owned by his ageing father. The shops sold mainly goods which are the object of "discretionary spending" – pet foods, gardening supplies – goods easily foregone be consumers short of money. The local economy had been severely rocked by the closure of a major employer – a nationalised industry whose regular massive losses had of course been financed by the taxes of self employed shopkeepers. Mr S. was also under pressure from local supermarkets which had received much help from the local council when locating in the town. Such help contrasted sharply with the behaviour of that council towards local shopkeepers like Mr S. When the council allowed an outside developer to build a bus station right across the town's main artery road it had as dramatic an effect on shop sales as the subsequent high unemployment from the closure of the steel plant.

These avoidable commercial disasters had also affected the trade of Mr Y who ran a bakery and two small shops, having worked as chief baker for the previous owners. The produce was popular among local shoppers but the strain of baking and running a business for the first time took its toll on his health. The business failed and now, in his late fifties, he faces debts of £18,000 on an income, after living costs, of £20 per month.

Mr S. was also unable to make a go of the business which he had risked a teaching career to take on. Bankruptcy now faces not only Mr S but also his father. Both have liabilities more than four times their assets. Both have lost their homes as the official receiver sets about raising funds to pay creditors. Mr S has delayed the realisation of his home since the Council has no alternative accommodation for him. His marriage has broken up and his brave attempt to rescue a family business is in ruins.

Mrs and Miss T, mother and dauther, kept a shop in Gateshead for many years. Recently they committed suicide. Their custom had been destroyed, virtually overnight, when the Gateshead Metro Centre, the largest shopping mall in Europe, opened. The Mall has been built on the banks of the Tyne which received the sudden windfall of designation as an Enterprise Zone. In such zones the State relieves business of all those State impositions which were responsible for decimating local business in the first place – taxes, rates, planning restrictions. The cost of these exemptions is of course borne by ordinary citizens – shopkeepers and their customers – whose taxes also

84

support the extensive tax privileges of the large quoted companies which now occupy the new mall.

Constrast the fate of these shopkeepers, who took considerable risks, served their fellow citizens in a competitive market and payed their taxes over many decades with those of similar age, social background and geographic region who worked for the State-owned coal and steel industries. These industries were for many years a net drain on the economy, their workers were not very productive and strikes were endemic. They produced goods which few wished to buy but for which all payed in their taxes, whether they consumed them or not.

When this burden became so great that even the State no longer dared pass the costs on to the innocent, then pits and steel works closed – abruptly. Here again the self employed, the non unionised, the ordinary citizen and his family, the shopkeepers – all were called upon to finance redundancy payments of up to £30,000 per man and early retirement pensions of up to 75% of final salary. Such is the price which the people pay to buy out the privileges of the monopolies which the State created.

The equivalents of Mr S, Mr Y and Mrs and Miss T in unionised State industry were powerful enough to lay down the conditions of their economic redundancy – even though they accelerated that redundancy through their own restrictive practices. There was no pressure on them to create, maintain, finance and manage their own business, no need to risk their homes to finance their trade, no trauma of bankruptcy. Rather they keep their assets, are well provided for and can spend the rest of their workings days on the golf course.

Even if the "equality" of which socialists speak were definable, even if it were just to force equal results out of unequal capacities, there would still remain the impossible myth that the State which takes on the universal power of a despot to impose this "equality" could ever be democratic.

When we examine the results of the State's compassion and democracy – more evident in the real world as the State's patronage and control – then we see an inequality more dangerous, pernicious and unchallengeable than the worst excesses of feudalism.

2 The Socialist effects of the Conservative State

Two young men in a northern town with very high unemployment each decided to set up their own business. Despite large grants, subsidies and rate holidays Mr. X established his business some miles away where he believed trade would be better. Mr. Y took advantage of the many subsidies and set up locally. Within a few months Mr. X was working 7 days a week and building up a solid financial base for his company. The subsidy and grant-laden Mr. Y was less industrious but was able to buy a rather sporty "company car". Not long after this splendid acquisition his company was bankrupt. Today, four years after Mr. X and Mr. Y started on the road of entrepreneurship Mr. X employs two others, has a substantial investment in printing machinery, is making good profits and has virtually no debt. And Mr. Y? He is employed by a local Government-financed agency (taxes paid by Mr. X) advising people how to set up businesses.

Two young ladies, well educated, experienced in business. One is married, has two children, works as a part time consultant and is a member of a group dedicated to placing "unwanted" children with foster parents. The other has never married, has borne three children by three different fathers, no longer works, has her own house and car and lives entirely from State support.

Two families in adjoining and identical houses on a Northern council estate. Family A, a retired couple, have always worked and saved and have acquired modest comforts out of their own resources. Family B, a young couple in their late twenties have never worked, make no particular efforts to find employment, have a well furnished house, colour television and two children. A few weeks ago their entire house was carpeted and curtained – by social security. They would indeed by very foolish to disturb this bliss by finding employment.

A businessman books into a conference on Japanese Trade, held in one of those gilded palaces habitually constructed by Northern socialist councils. Of the 240 delegates he discovers that approximately 180 are from local authorities and State funded "enterprise agencies". A Japanese diplomat is present and is somewhat perplexed to hear questions about enterprise zones, Government employment policy, new town development agencies and other parochial embarassments. Needless to say those businessmen not present – but finding more tangible ways of furthering Anglo-Japanese trade – would be overjoyed to see to what ends they pay their taxes. While they labour to build up wealth locally, the "public sector" uses their taxes to subsidise the more risky ventures of Tokyo shareholders.

In a northern town with 25% unemployment young men are taken in a council van to a local wood where work on a "youth opportunity" scheme is under way. They are not trained, they are not supervised, they are required to construct pathways through a wood. They are deposited in the morning and picked up again at night. In the same town other young men work as welders. In a good week "union rates", bonuses and overtime can mean between £500 and £900 per week for these elite and union protected few. Such is the equality of the distribution of wealth where State and Union power predominate.

A large Estate Agent in a Northern City is pleased to find office accommodation for a customer – a central location, prime office space. The office is fitted to the highest standards – expensive stairways, pictures, mahogany desks, quality carpets. This must indeed be a successful company, wealthy, profit-making, expanding. In fact it is the office of the Manpower Services Commission. No commercial business would begin the service of its fellow citizens with such pomp and expense but the State does so by taxing real wealth and job creation elsewhere in the economy. When the State is faced with a problem of economic adjustment it establishes organisations which, unlike the problem they were set up to solve, remain in perpetuity!

Government has overturned the natural laws of personal responsibility. It has rewarded those who make foolish decisions, subsidised those who fail, heavily taxed those who succeed, financed the birth of children to those who cannot even take care of themselves, taxed businessmen who have created jobs in order to finance the administration of grants and pseudo-employment and allowed Trade Unions to bring about the kind of exploitive inequality not seen since the early days of the industrial revolution.

If these are the actions of the benevolent State (under all parties) then it is time for the people to take away the power of that State. But did the electorate not twice ask Mrs Thatcher to

87

bring about just such a revolution? Every one of the above cases has its origins in legislation enacted or strengthened since 1979. Quis custodiet ipsos custodes?

3   Corporatism and the Crash

Before we accept the socialist diagnosis that the recent stockmarket crash is a capitalist free-market phenomenon let us consider the role of the State and socialist, or at least corporatist policies in precipitating this crisis. For the existence of Governments sympathetic to capitalism does not, as we know, mean an absence of socialism – as Conservative Governments in the UK have frequently demonstrated.

If Governments now seek to "coordinate" their international activities it was their "coordination" which has frustrated necessary change. If Governments now seek "economic stability" it was their instigation of rigid "stability" in currencies which prevented economic adaptation. If they now seek lower interest rates it was their policies on debt promotion which forced rates so high. If they now refer to the "fundamentals of the economy" then it was their fiscal and monetary distortions which unhinged stockmarkets from those fundamentals.

The more we have heard denials of the similarities between 1929 and the 1980's the more evident those similarities have become. Both the late 1920's and mid 1980's were periods of strong economic growth, recovery from inflation, a dominance of short term loans in an expanded debt market, the growth of trusts and institutional savings and investment and a high level of merger and takeover activity. Whereas the large discrepancies in wealth were class based in the 1920's today they are regionally and structurally significant (North – South, Inner City – suburbia, finance – production). The tragedy is that not only have all these characteristics returned *but they have been either caused or encouraged by Government itself.*

We see today with Government-boosted savings and investment what we previously saw with Government-and union-inspired inflation. The excessive activity of the central State has been the guilty party in both processes. It is as wrong for the State to promote capitalist investment or subsidise privatisation as it is to promote socialist trade unions or state industries. Such activities are not just wrong politically (using State power which derives from all to benefit a politically chosen few) but is economically inefficient. For if investment is rational and wise then rational people will invest without Government "incentives" – unless of course other "incentives" are attracting savings elsewhere. Naturally if, for instance, Government has taxed shareholders and given financial institutions tax allowances then ownership of shares will shift from the former to the latter – Government then provides another array of incentives to attract them back again. If Government, through non-commercial State production of energy, subsidises prices then consumers waste energy. Government therefore has to spend large sums promoting conservation. If Government prints and devalues money they can hardly object if banks, conscious of this now cheap and plentiful commodity, lend to doubtful companies and projects. (Even more funds are then required from Government to rescue both companies and banks.) If high capital and income taxes shift economic power to the centre it is not surprising that the peripheral regions decline – where capital goes, youth and entrepreneurship follow. In all these – and scores of other – cases Government has tried to reverse a damaging process which it instigated itself. The cost of these distortions and the enormous resources required to counter them seriously destabilise the economy, and such distortions, even after 10 years of a Government devoted to market forces, have not been significantly reduced overall. For while income taxes have fallen, overall taxation – like Government spending – has not fallen: companies have been privatised, but as monopolies, maintaining comfortable profits for Government to tax: the total Government subsidies for spending on pensions, mortgages, business investment etc have risen sharply, further distorting investment decisions, and boosting those very markets which are now in danger of collapse.

Although there is no general inflation there have ben classic signs of overheating in the markets for shares, property, art, industrial factory space, skilled workers and finance (100% mortgages even for the unemployed!)

As the monetarist economist Tim Congdon rightly pointed out these sectors have been "lead indicators" of inflation in the past so that either share and property prices will tumble (with proabable recession) or the pressure will feed through into higher inflation. This is the dilemma for most western Governments today. Having failed to tackle economic distortions in the real economy (indeed they have compounded them) they are left with inflation behind and recession ahead – perhaps it is too much to expect democratic Governments to change tack?

As in 1929 the critical period follows the share fall – will Governments relieve or compound the situation? The following guidelines might be observed:

- Supplying liquidity to rescue markets should not mean rescuing speculators or the shareholders in irresponsible financial institutions.
- The solutions to problems of economic change are rarely found in intergovernmental "coordination" or "stabilisation". International trade thrives on diversity, not uniformity and on changing not "coordinated" interest rates, currency levels etc.
- Macro-economic measures by central Governments cannot cure real economic problems – most of which have been caused by Government spending, borrowing, taxation or tax allowances, in the first place.
- While one of the main characteristics of the 1920's was social inequalities (leading to irresponsible capital owners), today the inequalities are regional, geographical and structural – usually caused or made worse by Government policies.
- Artificial Government boosts to savings and investment must be eliminated.
- Central Government should stop taxing and subsidising the regions into dependence on the centre.
- International trade imbalances must be solved by allowing currencies to find their market levels without Government guidance.
- Government should prevent or discourage on a permanent basis banks from lending to individuals to buy shares, and to corporations for high leveraged bids.
- The encouragement to property buyers to borrow for house purchase must be eliminated.
- A complete reappraisal of merger and takeover policy should be undertaken in the light of experience in the 1920's, 1970's and 1980's – all preceding catastrophic falls in share prices.

4 Conservative Socialism – Mortgage Interest Tax Relief

Preface

Mortgage Interest Tax Relief is a typical Government intervention – it provides profits for those who have not earned them, distorts the market which is subsidised, involves considerable costs for the rest of the economy, gives Government more power and the individual less, and brings about the opposite of what was intended. The ending of domestic rates presents a unique opportunity to abolish Mortgage Interest Relief since the same people who benefit from the former will suffer in roughly equal measure from the latter.

The assumed advantages for the Mortgage Interest subsidy are myths. Indeed the disadvantages are so pernicious and widespread that practically all the virtues of Conservatism – house building, home ownership and thrift – are in fact discouraged by the subsidy.

The case for change

By any standards the house price boom during the 1980s has been out of control. Prices have risen by a national average of over 30% during 1988, varying from 10% in Scotland to over 50% in East Anglia. If the Retail Prices Index including house prices, "inflation" would be over 9% pa.

However there are signs that the tide is turning and real house price falls have been recorded in central London. The potential collapse in house prices will be as dangerous for many families as the excessive price rises have been for the whole British economy.

The Government can scarely claim that it is powerless since the UK housing market is one of the most controlled and distorted markets in the world. Mortgage Interest Relief boosts the property market by about £5 billion per annum, Government inspired inflation subsidises (by devaluing) the debt raised by householders, capital gains on housing are free of tax and the decline in the private rented market – thanks to Government controls – forces the young and mobile into the (illogical) purchase of a house. The unnecessary seduction of so many into house ownership has led to record repossessions of houses by financial institutions.

	Repossessions		Loans 6-12 months in arrears	
	(figures in brackets are percentages of total loans)			
1979	2,530	(.048%)	8,420	(.16%)
1980	3,020		13,490	
1981	4,240		18,720	
1982	5,950		23,790	
1983	7,320		25,580	
1984	10,870		41,940	
1985	16,490		48,790	
1986	20,930		45,250	
1987	22,630	(.318%)	47,770	(.67%)
Real Increase		x6.5		x4

Source: Building Societies Association Bulletin

Since 1979 repossessions have risen 6.5 times and the number of loans 6 to 12 months in arrears has risen by four times – taking into account the increase in the number of loans. The cost of this naturally falls on the financial institutions, and therefore on depositors but Government bears the cost of another aspect of the housing market – by 1985/86 central Government was spending £360 per owner occupied house in social security payments to cover mortgage interest. This is a quite extraordinary subisidy, whereby the unemployed and the poor in employment who could never afford a house pay taxes (VAT at least) to finance the mortgage of the unemployed with a substantial asset!

To justify Mortgage Interest Relief for individuals by reference to interest deductions for business purposes is totally illegitimate. Commercial companies and individual businesses can deduct interest on *all* borrowing, not just borrowing for a specific purpose (which Government believes to more worthy!). but such is the position when Government chooses arbitrarily (and disastrously) to subsidise loans raised to buy homes. In addition companies have limited liability and they borrow to invest in income producing assets which are usually easily realisable whereas with no limited liablilty the mortgaged home produces no income and cannot be depreciated. Mortgages are financed by that dangerous business practice "borrowing short and lending long" – the position of the Building Societies in this Government subsidised merry-go-round.

The abolition of Mortgage Interest Relief (MIR) has always been opposed on four grounds:

1. That more money spent on housing will create more houses.
2. That it aids home ownership, particularly the first time buyer.
3. That it encourages responsible savings rather than wasteful expenditure.
4. That abolition would mean lower taxes for a few (who have no mortgages) and higher (effective) taxes for the many who do.

The first three claims can be demonstrated to be false and the fourth objection can be overcome with simultaneous abolition of the domestic rate. Few believe that Government subsidy is an aid to efficiency and the Government has rightly rejected thus argument for British industry, with beneficial results. A similar approach to the house mortgage market would be both logical and consistent.

It cannot be claimed that MIR aids home ownership since the biggest rise in home ownership occurred in the UK during the 1950s when MIR was cancelled out by Schedule A tax on house ownership. There is certainly no logic to the claim that a tax subsidy benefits first time buyers or families who need homes since the highest value of the relief is usually obtained by the single person with high earnings (and therefore the highest subsidy).

Year	Net advances for house purchases £m	First time buyers as % of total
1982	14,141	54.3
1983	14,525	52.8
1984	17,072	52.3
1985	19,116	53.0
1986	26,581	50.0
1987	n.a.	48.0

Source: Building Societies Association

In the late 1960s first time buyers accounted for 63% of all mortgages.

Home Ownership can only be promoted in the long run if more houses are built at prices which people can afford and the ownership of which they can sustain over their life time. With the average first time buyer now borrowing 90% of the price of his home the chances of such sustained ownership are small. The large amount of taxpayers money which the State has injected

94

into the housing market has not increased the amount spent on constructing homes for those who need them but instead has provided high taxpayers and existing householders with windfall profits. The UK has for many years spent less than half of the OECD average on house construction. A comparison of the growth in mortgage lending with capital spending on housing and loans per house completed demonstrate how a market subsidised and controlled by the State can get completely out of control.

Year	Mortgage lending £m	House capital spending % GDP	Net advance per house completed £
1969	858	5.0	2,260
1972	2,783	4.8	8,400
1975	3,650	4.4	11,330
1978	5,435	3.9	18,800
1982	13,623	2.2	77,400

Source: Financial Statistics

It is also claimed that MIR encourages savings for expenditure on a home rather than current expenditure on, say, drink, tobacco or holidays. But the reason why the British have not saved is because MIR subsidises *borrowing* – why save out of taxed income to buy a house when you can borrow with tax relief and rely on inflation to devalue that debt? The savings of the British have been decimated by inflation for some 25 years and the major contributor to the loss of monetary control at the root of inflation is excessive borrowing for house purchase. The ludicrous circle of failure must be broken.

The fourth objection can be largely met by taking advantage of the introduction of the Community Charge and the abolition of domestic rates. If rates and MIR were to be abolished simultaneously then there would be a rough balance between the loss of the tax allowance and the compensation removal of the rate burden. How the Treasury then chooses to reduce taxation, by reducing tax rates, raising thresholds or reducing indirect taxes will naturally affect different householders in varying degrees. However, the following two examples of a two bedroom flat in London and a large detached house in a rural area are indicative of the kind of balance which will result for many home owners.

A. *2 bedroom flat in London: Owner pays tax at 25%*

Rates abolished. Gain: £500
MIR loss £20,000 @ 12% 600   @ 8% 400   @ 4% 200
MIR loss £30,000 @ 12% 900   @ 8% 600   @ 4% 300

B. *Large detached house rural area. Owner pays tax at 40%*
Rates abolished. Gain: £1,100
MIR loss £30,000 @ 12% 1,440   @ 8% 960   @ 4% 480

Today's high interest rates which govern the level of MIR subsidy are a reflection of inflation and inflationary expectations. Much lower rates would result from a less inflationary environment to which the abolition of MIR would substantially contribute. As interest rates fall to 8% and then 4% (in the pre inflationary era historical average rates were c.3%) the MIR loss reduces.

Without the abolition of MIR the end of domestic rates will, on its own, certainly give a further boost to house prices since the payment of the Community Charge is unrelated to the possession of a house. The house price boom in the South East of England has already led to a reversal of one of the Government's major political successes – the sale of council houses. So expensive have the South East houses now become that there is an increasing demand for council housing – a more blatant example of political foot shooting would be hard to imagine.

There are even suggestions that certain Government departments may support a capital gains tax on housing. This is an all too typical response by the State to a problem of its own making – a solution of higher taxes, giving even more power and influence to that institution which is at the root of the problem it claims to be solving. In fact the profit which arises from house ownership is principally a "debt profit" and is not attached to the price of the house per se. The profit arises from inflation eating away at the value of the loan raised to buy the house. A £50,000 house sold 5 years later for £100,000 can only be replaced with a similar house costing £100,000. But if the £50,000 had been financed with £45,000 of debt than that debt would still be the same five years later even though the house price had risen to £100,000 that is only 45% of the house's value is now financed by the loan, instead of 90% at the outset. This enables the householder – even assuming a 70% debt ratio for his second home – to raise £105,000 to buy a new house costing £150,000 without having to save an additional penny! He then sits back and waits for another 5 years of inflation to reduce his new debt.

But this entire process of "trading up" on the basis of debt devaluation starts with the *first time buyer* and the Government incentive to borrow for house purchase. For more than 20 years first time buyers have been borrowing between 70% and 90% of

96

the purchase price of a house. There have been recent offers from financial institutions of 100% and 105% mortgages. The confidence of such institutions in the speculative and inflationary process which they assume will rescue them from this irresponsibility is based on the Government's track record of intervention in the housing market.

Although it is not unreasonable for the young to borrow against their prospective life time's income or finance a capital asset like a house with a long term loan it is also not unreasonable to expect all house buyers to *save* a fair proportion of the price of their house. It is the Government subsidised assumption that debt is the first step to home ownership which fuels the house price spiral. The Royal Institute of Chartered Surveyors recently took fright:

> "Prices in London could fall as first time buyers are unable to get a foot on the ladder" (Financial Times).

Government, banks, building societies, surveyors and especially recent home owners fear that if the irresponsible inflationary spiral is not fed frequent tax subsidies the whole system could collapse with loss of homes, insolvency and loss of votes! A similar psychosis fuelled the inflation of the 1920s and the early 1970s. The Government must tackle its subsidies to the housing market, the official (MIR) and the unofficial (inflation) which entice the first time buyer and provide him with the funds to pay the excessive "first time sellers" price and so on up the spiral.

Economic consequences
Between 1969 and 1982 the inflation adjusted increase in net advances for housing was over 1200% while the increase in the stock of dwellings in the same period was a mere 13%. The only way to increase home ownership is to increase the supply of suitable dwellings. Neither this aim nor the intention to help first time buyers is furthered by a tax incentive to borrow. If there is any excuse at all for subsidy it must surely be for house *building* rather than debt funded house *purchase*.

In the United Kingdom house ownership by the under 25s is the highest of any democracy:

UK	30%
Canada	17%
Australia	23%
Holland	16%
France	7%
Germany	4%

Source: OECD

If this position had arisen out of rational choice undistorted by the activities of Government it might be a praiseworthy acheivement – a signal of a highly stable and prosperous country. But young people in Britain happen to be among the poorest, least mobile and most unemployed in any advanced industrial country. Many are seduced into house ownership and high debt by the tax subsidy, others are forced into home ownership because the private rented sector has been distorted by Government leglislation and, in effect taxed by the subsidy to home ownership. Having bought a house they are trapped when unemployment strikes and house prices in their area fall. Even if they manage to sell their house they will find themselves unable to afford a property in an area with better job prospects and so remaining unemployed may well be preferable to moving.

Much of the very large differences in house prices between more and less prosperous areas is due in no small measure to the higher subsidy in rich areas with high tax payers. If there were no MIR the difference between house prices would be less, the rented sector would aid mobility and the young would not be seduced into mistaken and inflexible house ownership.

If there is one certain result of a financial windfall it is that it will be wasted by its recipients. The nearly £5 billion per annum which the State lavishes on those who have house mortgages finds its way swiftly into the hands of those who provide mortgages and build houses. The Building Societies which are often erroneously described as "non-profit making" take their profits in the form of higher salaries and less efficiency. We can compare Building Society managment expenses in 1960, when the MIR was balanced by Schedule A tax on housing with 1983 after 21 years of a net mortgage subsidy from 3.2% in 1969 to

5.1% in 1983. Considering the advances in office automation and electronic information systems this decline in efficiency is quite remarkable.

BUILDING SOCIETIES
Management Expenses and Depreciation as percentage of Advances 1960-1983

Year	Mortgages Advanced £m	Expenses £m	Expenses as % of Advances
1960	560	18	3.2
1961	546	20	3.6
1962	613	22	3.5
1963	849	25	2.9
1964	1,043	28	2.6
1965	955	32	3.3
1966	1,245	37	2.9
1967	1,463	42	2.8
1968	1,590	49	3.1
1969	1,559	57	3.6
1970	1,954	68	3.4
1971	2,705	85	3.1
1972	3,630	102	2.8
1973	3,513	119	3.4
1974	2,945	145	4.9
1975	4,908	197	4.0
1976	6,183	237	3.8
1977	6,745	297	4.4
1978	8,808	363	4.1
1979	9,002	449	4.9
1980	9,503	590	6.2
1981	12,005	732	6.1
1982	15,033	815	5.4
1983	19,357	996	5.1

Source: Building Societies Association

MIR has its biggest impact in times of high inflation when, because much of the "interest" paid in effect represents capital repayments, mortgage holders recieve tax relief on their repayments! Also when interest rates are high – usually in an attempt to defeat inflation – the Government subsidy is worth much more. It is interesting to note in the table above the 70% rise in mortgages advanced between 1962 and 1964 – the first two years of the effective *net* subsidy. The biggest rise in the costs of the Building Societies was between 1972 and 1982 when inflation was at its height and to the official MIR the unofficial subsidy of inflation gave further stimulus to the profitable game of housing debt.

The other beneficiaries of the Government's largesse, housebuilders, have not only taken higher profits from fewer houses but their productivity has declined rapidly. The builders, Laing, noted that the same house built in the 1930s in one month today takes 2 months while the industry average is 5 months!

So the Government subsidy to the individual householder serves only to raise house prices, reduce the number of houses built and allow mortgage providers and housebuilders to become less efficient while making higher profits.

The recent pressure on bank lending, money supply and hence inflation has come principally (even more than in the 1970s) from the personal sector and mortgage lending in particular, helping to make the profitability of housing debt a self-fulfilling prophecy.

The effect of the mortgage interest subsidy and its distorting influence on general economic managment was demonstrated graphically when the Chancellor was recently torn between lower interest rates to prevent an excessive rise in Sterling and higher rates to reduce inflationary pressures in the domestic economy. By abolishing MIR both objectives could have been achieved simultaneously since external investors in Sterling would get no higher rate of interest but internal borrowers would have to pay more.

The end of the house price boom

Like all speculative booms, and especially those instigated or encouraged by the State, the house price spiral will probably turn into a price collapse. Several new elements in the market are likely to reverse a 30 year process, although the full effects may be delayed for a year ot two.

1. Lower inflation in the 1980s has led to a rise in private sector house building – house *supply* is up.
2. The "baby boom" house buyers now have their houses and the 1960s and 1970s generation are fewer (school places today, house needs tomorrow) – house *demand* is lower.
3. Real interest rates are very high while lower tax rates mean the tax allowance on mortgages is worth less
4. The new qualification for Business Expansion Scheme subsidy for "assured tenancies" will rejuvenate the long dead private rented sector. For the first time in 80 years there will be a real option of selling and renting and Britain will experience the phenomenon known in other European countries where a flourishing rented sector exists – falling house prices.

100

It is therefore vital that the Government prepares for a real house price fall and ensures that those who have been seduced by Government subsidies, allowances and inflation can find a way out of a trap which is already being sprung. Many unsophisticated first time buyers have been attracted into house ownership through the price boom, easy credit, subsidised council house sales and tax relief. Perhaps the most irresponsible aspect was the Government's own encouragement of a five month buying spree for double mortgage holders sharing a house. Needless to say house sellers and estate agents saw these buyers coming (with their perishable subsidy) and a further twist to the house price spiral ensued. These double mortgage householders will have burdened themselves with high debt, contracted at a time of artificially low interest rates as Stirling was manipulated. With rising interest rates and lower house prices the Government must ensure that financial institutions do not behave as irresponsibly when householders get into trouble as they did when those same householders were showered with excessively easy credit.

The Government inspired diversion of savings from commercial investment into housing speculation over many decades has benefited housebuilders, Building Societies, existing home owners and high tax payers. It has not helped those who own no house nor encouraged the expansion of the housing stock but it has served to confirm the advantages of inflation by providing further incentives for debtors.

The policy of successive Governments has wrought the kind of inflated, highly speculative, non-productive activity in the housing market which was typical of the entire British economy in the 1960s and 1970s. That after nearly 10 years of a Government devoted to market principles, such conditions should still apply can only be regarded as an economic and political failure.

MIR is a typical Government intervention. It brings about the opposite of what is intended and at considerable cost in terms of economic efficiency. It:

- costs nearly £5 billion per annum.
- promotes inflation and therefore leads to less saving.
- raises house prices without increasing the amount spent on house building.
- has no demonstrably positive effect on home ownership.

101

- promotes the construction of house types suitable for higher rate tax payers (often single) but not for families who need housing.
- seduces many of the youngest and least well off into unsustainable house ownership.
- actively discriminates against the first time buyer.
- increases the economic differences between regions.
- distorts capital markets and prevents labour mobility.
- raises interest rates above their natural level, thereby serving as a tax on industry.
- makes macro-economic management far more difficult.

Conclusions

1. Mortgage Interest Relief discourages practically all the virtues of Conservatism – house building, home ownership and thrift.

2. MIR and the domestic rates should be abolished simultaneously, thus roughly balancing the disadvantage of one with the advantage of the other. Any saving to the Exchequer from these steps and the introduction of the Community Charge should be used to reduce taxation – including indirect taxes.

3. There should be no question of introducing capital gains tax on the sale of the principal residence – this is a typical response of Government to a market distorted by its own policies.

4. The Government should prepare for a major fall in house prices and ensure that financial institutions do not discourage early loan repayments and do not delay or disguise the true interest cost of house loans.

5. Tax relief on "only £30,000 of debt" is in fact the golden source of the profit on which the house price spiral depends.

6. If a Conservative Government does not abolish MIR in order to *reduce* taxation, a future Government will do so in order to *raise* taxes.

5 Government-guided Expenditure

It is one of the great ironies of political debate that money spent by Government is called "public expenditure" while money spent by the public is not even classified!

Government expenditure varies as a percentage of Gross National Product from about 30% to over 50% in the industrial democracies. Most Governments are now reducing that share of "public expenditure" which they channel through the State. The most radical changes are being made by President Reagan with maximum tax rates of 27% and the elimination of most allowances. Nigel Lawson is rightly worried that unless similar measures are taken in the United Kingdom some of our most able and high earning businessmen will prefer a country where the public's expenditure bears a closer relationship to their actual earnings!

Government expenditure is well catalogued – both the totals and the various items of expenditure. However there is an equally important kind of Government expenditure which is not usually so classified which I term Government-guided expenditure. We are accustomed to Government taking taxes and using them to build roads and purchase goods for our national defence. But what of those occasions when the State returns our taxes to us? A pointless excersise at first sight. But the State has a purpose in this circular activity – it only hands back our money if we spend it (and more!) on those things which the State regards as particulary worthy. Not surprisingly we find this means, inter alia, political donations and investment in Government bonds!

Tax is returned if we pay interest on a house loan. Tax is returned if we invest through Pension Funds and Life Assurance (the latter still costs the Treasury money despite abolition in 1984) and more is returned if we invest in Business Expansion Schemes. The tables demonstrate the extent of this "guided expenditure" in the USA and the United Kingdom. If you choose not to spend money in these ways you will pay more tax than those who do. I have not included in the definition of "guided expenditure" allowances for "what people are" as it were – for instance disability allowance, married man's allowance or *general* corporate tax thresholds. I include only those allowances which encourage people to do or become things which they might otherwise not choose, for instance house loan purchasers, investors in Government stock, life assurance or share options.

As can be seen from the tables, while direct Government expenditure as a percentage of GDP in the United Kingdom was 43.8% in 1985/86, a further 5.2% of GDP (£18.4 billion) was spent to guide expenditure by the public into ways more acceptable to Government. In the USA in 1986 Federal Government expenditure as a percentage of GDP was 23.8% (this figure excludes expenditure by individual States) but a further 3.26% of GDP (139 billion) was spent on guided expenditure.

Naturally some of these expenditure patterns would have occurred anyway. On the other hand much of the Government's largesse in the USA and the UK is directed at interest payments where a given relief is considerably "geared up" in actual expenditure terms. In other words if tax relief produces a 30% decrease in the real cost of interest on a loan of £30,000 then a loan of £40,000 can be contracted – and spent – with no extra cost to the consumer.

The really critical element in the economic development of a country is not so much the balance between Government and public expenditure or the tax level itself but the extent to which the country's commercial assets and skills are used to meet the needs of rational consumers. If Government guides consumer's expenditure in ways which are not rational then producers will be seduced into poor investment and superfluous production. Just such a process causes long term damage to the structure of any economy – one of the reasons for instance why the UK has a proliferation of Building Societies, excessively-paid insurance salesman and pension fund managers and yet a yawning trade gap in manufactured goods.

The Americans have recognised this and are reducing "guided expenditure" as well as tax rates. The question is: has the British Government the courage to eliminate these more covert forms of Government expenditure? Or does a Conservative Government believe Socialism is acceptable – provided of course that Conservatives are pulling the levers of State control?

These are two occasions when the voter should watch his wallet – where the Socialist says he will "help" and when the Conservative offers an "incentive".

104

GOVERNMENT-GUIDED EXPENDITURE

1985/86 – UNITED KINGDOM	Cost to Exchequer (million pounds)
Employers and employees contributions to occupational pension schemes	3,600
Investment income of pension schemes	3,500
Lump sum payments to pensioners	1,000
Life Assurance premiums (contracts made before 14.3.84)	640
Mortgage interest relief	4,750
Approved profit sharing schemes	60
Share option schemes	11
Business Expansion Scheme	75
Interest on National Savings Certificates	450
British Government Securities where owner not normally resident in the UK	280
Gains arising on disposal of Life Assurance policies	100
Gains arising on disposal of main residence	2,500
Stamp duty exemptions for transfer of Government stock and local authority loans	1,500
	Total £18,466m
	GDP £360,000m
Cost of Guided Spending 5.2% at GDP	

1986 USA	Cost to Treasury (Million dollars)
Housing and meals for millitary personnel	2,400
Relief on profits for export sales	1,700
Housing allowances for Americans abroad	2,400
Various energy related credits	860
Private forestry	50
Deductions for Life Assurance companies	1,420
Accelerated depreciation buildings, machinery	32,600
Deferral of capital gains on home sales	2,600
Interest on owner occupied housing	2,100
Deductibility of mortgage interest	27,500
Deductibility of interest, consumer credit	16,000
Interest on Life Assurance savings	5,300
Shipping indefinite tax referal	40
Education	4,075
Health – insurance contributions, hospital bonds etc	39,700
Political contributions	290
Deferral of income on US savings bonds	850
	Total 139,885m
	GDP 4,285,000m
Cost of Guided Spending: 3.26% of GDP	

6 The Community Charge

Although rebellions by Conservatives in both Houses of Parliament on the Bill introducing the Community Charge have failed, the size of the Commons rebellion should at least cause the Government to reconsider the aims of this legislation.

Changes can still be made without compromising the basic principle of relating political choice to financial responsibility – which is accepted by most of those who have organised and supported these poorly constructed rebellions.

It is significant that opponents of the Community Charge call it a Poll Tax, for to many it seems as unacceptable to relate taxation to the "the ability to vote" as it is to divorce the Community Charge from "the ability to pay".

Very few politicians in national and local Government understand the complexities of Local Authority finance. Those who do find it chaotic and those who don't find it unfair.

At the institutional level the struggle between HM Treasury and Local Authority finance departments is as "petty political" as between national Governments and the European Commission – that it has less to do with political representation of the people than with the institutional defence of bureaucratic privilege. There is no greater privilege than the power to raise taxes and no greater source of patronage than the power to decide who shall be given "allowances" to avoid those taxes! It is largely because HM Treasury has fought tooth and nail to defend this exclusive privilege that a Government which was already showing signs of excessive centralisation has allocated to itself 74% of the revenue raising for Local Government and dictated the Community Charge to raise the rest.

The Community Charge is opposed by many members of Parliament because they claim there is a very limited concession to "ability to pay". There is however no such concession for payments for postage stamps, televison licence and car tax (costing respectively 18p, £62.50 and £100) and yet these are not the subject of regular Parliamentary rebellions. With the Community Charge therefore it seems to be not just a question of principle but of the *amount* of the charge.

Those who drafted the legislation have not grasped the critical distinction between a charge and a tax and the two different kinds of expenditure which each form of revenue raising should properly finance. Taxes which are based on ability to pay (ie a percentage of the payers income) should finance a national service like education or social services from which not everyone will benefit directly or equally but the extent and application of which is a responsibility reserved to itself by Central Government – however much Local Government may administer that service. A Charge on the other hand should be used to finance *local* services from which all could or do benefit – library service, refuse collection, sewerage. The charge for such services should be flat rate, just as the cost of postage does not rise with the income of the buyer.

An analysis of Local Government expenditure shows that no more than 14% could be described as local services which the Community Charge should cover. The remaining 86% of locally adminstered expenditure covers "national services" – education (50%) social services (10.8%) Law and Order (15.6%) Transport (7.2%) and Housing (2.5%).

However the Community Charge under the Government's Bill will account not for 14% of Local Authority expenditure but 26%. In other words individuals will pay through a charge for 12% more than they should. If the extra 12% could be financed by central Government (and hence "ability to pay" taxation) then the two problems will be solved. The amount which each individual will have to pay will be substantially reduced and the flat rate charge will be justified by reference to *local* services available to all in the local community – presumably a reasonable definition of "Local Government"!

If this seems to contribute, even more than the present revenue raising proposals to the move towards political and fiscal centralisation then this is no more than the logic of "payment and responsibility" would demand. For why should the payers of the Community Charge be financially accountable for that which their elected representatives are not logically responsible – ie the 86% of local spending which is decided nationally rather than locally?

There is no doubt that the United Kingdom has already suffered from excessive centralisation in London and the South East of industrial, legal, political and financial power. But if Government denies to local authorities both real power over education, law and order etc *and taxation* (as opposed to charge) powers then it has no choice but to fund directly a greater proportion of Local Government spending than under the present proposals.

The excess burden of the Community Charge on so many has already been admitted by the Government, since many exemptions for the poorly paid have been introduced. Massive exemptions are a poor beginning to any system of revenue raising. Such exemptions, of which there are already far too many in the United Kingdom, exacerbate the "poverty trap". They make it far more difficult for the poor to break their dependence on the State since their first employment opportunity – or promotion – which brings them above the exemption threshold means a sudden tax burden. A poorly defined Community Charge increases the value of those exemptions and increases State dependence.

Recent changes in social security, which reduced rate rebates, will have convinced many more voters of the *real* unfairness of domestic rates – and therefore of the relative attraction of the Community Charge. If the above amendments to the leglisation are accepted by Government then the broad base of popular support which any legislation must enjoy will be forthcoming.

7 What Governments Cannot Do

The Government has decided to allow Sterling to find its market level, instead of manipulating the currency and courting inflation or recession. This is no mere technicality – it is a major philosophical change in the Government's approach to international economics.

That market philosophy which has served the country well domestically is now being applied more consistently to our external affairs. Perhaps this may presage moves against other forms of international "statism" – trade manipulation, UN and World Bank intervention and IMF financial manipulation.

There are already signs of unaccustomed modesty from international agencies – the Louvre agreement has accepted the catastrophic fall of the US dollar which the participating Governments had decided to prevent and the G7 agreements to "stabilise" currencies has accepted a sudden rise in the pound with equanimity.

The greatest failures of the State arise out of its purest motives. Governments wish to "coordinate", "bring stability", "encourage growth" or "raise demand". But these laudable aims are already being realised by the people in general – in their free individual and corporate activities. These activities are reflected in changing prices, costs, interest rates, the language of economic and social communication – a communication independent of Governments. The most dangerous and now the most pervasive form of State intrusion upon this communication between people is to be found in international economics. This is best illustrated by some recent statements by Finance Ministers, Governments and the communiques of international meetings:

> "Britain should join the EMS in order to stabilise the Pound".
> "Central Banks believe stability of exchange rates desirable".
> "Germany should adopt more expansive growth policies".
> "All the leaders endorsed America's call for greater coordination of economic policies".

"The Treasury Secretary is pressing for the adoption of economic indicators to which world policy makers can look when deciding changes in monetary and fiscal policy".

Such statements are the staple diet of international "Statesmanship" and actions based upon them bring about the very instability which Governments seek to avoid.

Changes in trade patterns, balance of payments, currency levels and economic growth are welcome signs of creative and intelligent human activity. Such spontaneous signals are both reliable and democratic. If the Pound is weak it is because the UK is "printing money" or because our trading position is deteriorating. If the Government tries to "stabilise" (in this case raise) the currency level then the international and domestic signal "no change" is at a variance with reality "balance of payments weakening". Domestic consumers will be misled, imports will continue to rise and exporters will be at a disadvantage. Similarly if the German Government is persuaded to "expand the economy" then it will manipulate credit conditions to give the impression that there is more money available, that goods are cheaper and costs lower than is in fact the case. The rational German consumer and investor is therefore deceived into irrational and wasteful activities. The backlash is inevitable and *long run* growth will be no higher than if Government had done nothing – except that the sudden fluctuations will have caused wastage, higher unemployment and higher indebtedness.

Trade is about differences. No one trades with someone who has exactly the same goods at the same price and at the same time as himself. Individuals differ as do companies and countries – hence trade is profitable and mutually advantageous. Traders rely on accurate signals of these differences and the commercial opportunities which arise from them. Any third party such as Government or international agency which reacts universally to market signals by "deciding changes in monetary and fiscal policies" or by "coordinating international growth" destroys those signals and (seemingly) reduces those differences. This disguise invalidates the market mechanism on which the wealth of all – even, eventually Governments' – depends.

It is one matter to have a single reliable language for communication it is quite another to iron out the differences between words and expect communication to take place – but that is exactly the effect of Government intervention in markets.

110

Spontaneous economic activity is not perfect, no more than linguistic communication always brings about immediate understanding, but free and responsible trade in a market is an *optimising process*. If internationalists reject certain *states* as unacceptable and enforce their procrustean view of the world then that optimising process breaks down. No such process can ever survive the intrusion of absloute power – and only Governments have that power. Absolute powers do not need to communicate (they just impose) but the people do and for that they require an unmanipulated *economic* language. Is it too much to expect that our international Statesmen will learn the lessons of the market which some of their number have applied with profit at home?

8 Why does Mrs Thatcher tax Conservatives?

Why does a Conservative Government tax individual Conservatives in order to subsidise corporations, financial institutions and even socialists? Overall taxation is higher after 10 years of Conservative "market economics" than under a socialist Government. In addition "tax expenditures" – a form of State spending – have risen as the Treasury has added to Mortgage Interest and Pension contribution reliefs a new batch of concessions – the Business Expansion Scheme and Personal Equity Plans.

Such tax reliefs require considerable administration and are usually run by banks, accountants and solicitors - not quite the enterprising, flexible individualist approach which a Conservative Government is, in theory, trying to promote.

An individual can now invest £4800 per annum in a PEP scheme free of income and capital gains tax. Typical Conservative voters have been investing in stocks and shares on their own account for years and have been taxed severely for the privilege. But this new tax free investment is only available to them if they hand over their savings to a fund manager, usually by way of a broker. If you had just invested the maximum £3000 for the financial year ending in April 1989 a broker would have charged £52.00, the initial "plan charge" would have been £51.75 and the annual charge £43.10. If you had chosen 3 separate shares for you PEP you would have been charged £15 and had you had the temerity to ask to attend shareholders meetings and receive report and accounts relating to your investments a further £50 would have been charged. The total of £211.85 would account for 7.1% of your investment. This would certainly wipe out any potential gain, indeed allowing for inflation there would have been a substantial loss – and for this a Conservative Government gives tax allowances.

When the State gives a subsidy then middlemen cream off that subsidy and the individual gains little, indeed he suffers because he has lost control of his own investments. If the Prime Minister wishes to reduce taxes on share investments then let her do so simply, openly and honestly for the individual not for the benefit of remote and largely incompetent institutions. No wonder that the percentage of shareholdings held by individuals has halved since 1979.

Why does the Prime Minister take £6 billion per annum in taxes largely from her own supporters and then hand it back again on the condition that they incur debt to buy a house? Conservatism is about thrift and personal responsibility, not contracting large debts and giving larger profits to Building Societies, Banks and Estate Agents.

Why are Conservatives, who are perfectly capable of providing for their old age, forced to hand over their savings to pension funds in order to avoid taxes? At least Harold Wilson recognised the enormous power of the Pension Funds (and Mr Benn looked on them with glee as a source of coerced investment) Mrs Thatcher seems oblivious to the dangers of centralised institutional capital and of her own Government's role in strengthening those bases of financial power – at the expense of individual Conservatives.

Company cars are another example of corporate power and patronage. An ordinary citizen must buy his car out of taxed income. The self employed receives a car allowance against his own income but he may have to pay income tax on the sale of his car. A typical company manager however need not find a penny of his own money and will pay no tax when he changes cars. The tax on the use of a free car is derisory. No wonder 42% of cars entering London in the morning are not owned by their drivers but by their corporate employers.

A legislative privilege given to Trade Unions – the closed shop – is a "tax" on the company, consumers and other workers who do not enjoy that privilege. An "enterprise zone" gives large tax privileges to companies who move in but is an effective tax – indeed a double tax – on those companies outside the zone. Firstly the taxes of companies outside pay for the subsidies and secondly the prices of goods made inside the zone can undercut goods made outside – hence a "tax" on profits. The taxes of many Conservative shopkeepers are today providing profits for chain stores in enterprise zones and Government funded development agencies provide many socialist councils with the power and patronage reminiscent of the 1960's.

For many years Conservatives saved out of high taxed income to invest in shares in British companies. A large proportion of the taxes went towards losses of State industries whose workers

113

qualified for large redundancy payments. When Mrs Thatcher's Government privatised these concerns the employees were given shares at much reduced prices and a quick profit was engineered by underpricing the share issue. A similar process was at work when council houses were sold to their tenants for large (now 50%) discounts – many have been sold at a considerable profit. Who has paid for this largesse for unionised workers and council tenants? – typical Conservative voters, whether as householders, taxpayers or shareholders.

Although the Chancellor has introduced many welcome changes to inheritance tax, any individual will, on death, lose to the State 40% of any "wealth" which exceeds the value of a one bedroom flat in London. The basis of the Conservative philosophy is the responsibility of the individual within his family, community and nation. Thrift and the preservation of the value of money are not for one generation but for families. Indeed *responsible wealth creation through public service is usually possible only through the accumulated work of several generations*. Of course pools winners, pop singers, night club owners and property speculators can make a quick profit in a very short time – but they are hardly the backbone of an educated, responsible and enterprising nation. There are many Johnny-come-latelys to the Conservative ranks who have benefited from such windfalls while the family wealth of generations of long standing Conservatives has been taxed by the State and wasted by the spendthrift. The Prime Minister rightly complains that "active citizens" are not engaged in local communities, charities, politics and the arts. No wonder – those who understood such obligations have been and continue to be decimated by taxes while the pop singer in the Manor House today has little time or inclination.

Conservatives understand the value of saving and investment. Socialists prefer Government borrowing and spending. After all if you deny the historical significance of individual responsibility and family continuity why not burden future generations with debt and spend on yourself today? The result of that philosophy was inflation – the most insidious attack on the Conservative virtue of thrift. We remember when real returns on capital were negative (and the resulting profits to Government enormous). Today we have real returns but only at the cost of very high interest rates which give a further boost to the "here and now", the quick profit, the speculative venture rather than long term investment in the organic growth of business, families and individual education which are the hallmarks of the Conservative philosophy. In the pre inflationary era interest rates were about 3% per annum ie it would have taken 33 years for interest paid to equate to the value of the loan. Today it takes only 7 years so that the return on today's investment must be quick and that means the kind of risky, superficial, mass market trivia which Conservatives know do *not* represent economic or social progress.

So do we have a Conservative Government or is Mrs Thatcher showing distinct socialist and corporatist tendencies? Does she believe that individuals should be taxed in order to finance the whims of the State and receive tax allowances only if they turn their individual savings into corporate investments?

Privatisation has spawned too many large and irresponsible quasi monopolies and we have witnessed the ludicrous sight of individual investors with their taxed savings competing for privatisation shares against their own (untaxed) money in the hands of institutional investors. Their profit on those shares has been highest where they, as consumers, were most exploited-by the very monopoly in which they had invested.

Corporatism is the Conservative's vice. It is of complete indifference to the man in the street whether he is faced by remote and privileged State industry, financed by taxes, or remote and privileged corporate power subsidised by tax allowances. Mrs Thatcher has reduced the former but has regrettably increased the latter. There are many ways to tax the people and Mrs Thatcher has found rather too many ways of taxing her own supporters.

9 The Economic Paradoxes of Excessive Government

It should be no surprise, when Governments have systematically contradicted those who voted for them that even in economics, completely contradictory statements can both be true. Interest rates are too high for foreign investors in Sterling and our currency is substantially over valued as a result. But it is equally true to say that for the British home buyer interest rates are too low and this is the principal reason for excessive consumer demand and higher inflation.The combination of these two effects is a deteriorating balance of payments deficit.

What is interest? In the days when Government did not control or influence 50% of the nation's spending and did not seek to manipulate the value of the people's money, interest used to be distinct from capital. It was taxed as income and the capital on which interest was paid retained its value. The average man could assume that interest and capital were what the dictionary said they were and money conformed to the promise on the Government's banknotes.

However for several decades, and particularly since the late 1950's money has become the principal method employed by British (and many other) Governments to manipulate economic and social relations, to tax the people without Parliamentary approval and to provide a source of profit for the institutions of the State.

As a result interest, capital, savings and many other basic economic definitions have either lost their meanings altogether or now mean something completely different. For if an investor receives 13% "interest" on £1000 today only about 5.5% is really interest. At today's inflation rate of 7.5% his £1000 will have lost £75 of its original value after one year. So this £75 (out of a total interest payment of £130) is not interest at all – it is a return of a portion of the original investment or loan. Needless to say the Government does not see matters this way and will tax the investors £130 "interest" at, let us say, 25% or £32.50. £75 is the return of the investors own capital, £32.50 is tax and the remainder – £22.50 – represents the return of 2.2%. At a 40% tax rate the return would have been 0.3%

Had the same individual *borrowed* £1000 to buy a house the reverse would have been the case. His £1000 debt would have been *reduced* by £75, he would have received a tax *allowance* of £32.50 and the loan would have cost 2.2% or a mere 0.3% at the higher rate of tax.

No wonder Britain has become a nation of individual debtors just as the Government is reducing its debt.

During the high inflation of the 1960's and 1970's negative real interest rates were common. In the pre inflationary era about 3% was usual. But today both inflation and real interest rates are high. Needless to say it is Government which is the major beneficiary. It succeeds in raising excessive taxes from the saver when real interest rates and inflation are high and it raises high taxes and drastically reduces its own debt when inflation is high and interest rates negative.

As we have seen the Government extracts 11.3% (or 84%) of the present "interest rate" of 13.5% by means of the official tax and the unofficial tax-inflation. This Government profit is now being used to repay its own debt. When the State benefits, the people and country often lose. Mortgage Interest Relief induces individuals to high levels of debt and contributes to higher inflation but this combination aids Government revenues. As VAT has accounted for an even higher proportion of tax revenues we witness a relative indifference of Government to our balance of payments deficit. After all VAT is more ubiquitous, and easier to collect than income tax and it is paid on imports just as on home produced goods.

Just as Government taxes and inflation give the State an interest in individual debtors so those same elements drive the individual to debt. For how can the individual acquire capital quickly (or even slowly)? Inflation makes saving a waste of time, significant inheritance is forbidden, capital gains are taxed as income. Debt is the obvious solution – and there is no better object for purchase with that debt than a house where tax relief can be maximised.

The Government is at present struggling, through the weapon of interest rates to bring home to a spendthrift nation that there is a balance of payments crisis. And yet the higher interest rates go, the larger the Mortgage Interest subsidy to debtors, the smaller the effect of the interest rise, the higher the pound goes, the cheaper imports become and the more expensive exports become. No wonder there is little effect on house spending, inflation and the chronic balance of payments deficit.

Mortgage Interest Relief makes the interest rate weapon self defeating in another important respect. House *builders* do not get the benefit of MIRAS – the system whereby individual mortgage holders get immediate cash reduction of their monthly interest payments. The building industry pays the higher interest rates in full with the inflationary effect that fewer houses are *built* while housing *demand* remains, relatively, bouyant.

So the Government, which in theory represents the people, is paying off its debts largely from the profits it makes from the peoples increasing indebtedness. Interest rates for the building industry are too high for but for home buyers too low. For the level of the Pound and the health of our balance of payments interest rates are too high but for domestic demand control they are too low. The people suffer directly (fewer jobs) from a balance of payments deficit but VAT on imports cushions the effect on Government. The Government blames industry for paying their employees too much and yet it has been Government money printing which provides the funds and the closed shop – still virulent after 10 years of Mrs Thatcher – which extracts the high wages. Foreign goods are too cheap for British consumers but the Treasury makes them even cheaper by driving up Sterling with high interest rates which stifle home production.

All these paradoxes are caused by Government and its myriad interventions in the economy. Whatever happened to the Conservative Government which believed in market pricing, non manipulation of currencies, fiscal neutrality and lower taxes? The Government itself has become a paradox – it believes in market Conservatism but practises interventionist Socialism.

Although Nigel Lawson, after a brilliant start at the Treasury, lapsed into loss of monetary control and international collective manipulation of currencies he is after all only the nation's "Finance Director". For the plethora of tax allowances, high Government spending, pension privileges and inducements to debt we must blame the nation's "Managing Director" next door.

CONCLUSION

As I write the conclusion to these essays on Government and its dubious democratic credentials, British and American air travellers find themselves united in criticising their respective Governments. Both Governments were given detailed warnings of an attempt to blow up a Pan Am jet travelling from Frankfurt to the United States during December 1988. At the same time a terrorist arrested in Frankfurt was found to be in possession of a plastic explosive concealed in a radio/cassette player. Despite the extraordinarily precise warning of an attack neither the airline and the airports involved nor the UK and American Governments acted speedily or responsibly.

There are two disturbing aspects to these events which are significant for the general analysis of democratic accountability contained in these pages. They demonstrate that the first instinct of Government and political representatives is the preservation of their own lives and privileges rather than those they represent. The American Government relayed the intelligence reports of a Pan Am bomb threat to their diplomats in Europe. These servants of the State made alternative travel arrangements – indeed that is why there were many empty seats when the plane left Frankfurt. No similar information was made available to the American public or the citizens of any other nation. The British Government equally failed to give any public warning despite the detailed intelligence information. It also emerged that there is no equipment at British airports capable of "sniffing" plastic explosive like the notorious "Semtex" responsible for the Lockerbie disaster. (This explosive, incidentally, is manufactured in communist Czechoslovakia – in a State explosives factory.) However such equipment has long been available and the firm which makes it has been trying in vain to persuade British airports and the British Government to install it. There is in fact one functioning system in place. Is it located where the public or sensitive offices could be protected? – at airports, train or bus stations, at army bases, at the Ministry of Defence? No – it is in the House of Commons, guarding our guardians.

The essays in this book have analysed many aspects of the relationship between the individual and the State and the increasingly tenuous connection between Government and Democracy. The cases of Government failure and political distortion of the Democratic will are varied but the lessons for Democracy and the free and responsible individual are, I hope, clear.

State aid tends to aid the State, not the individual who needs support nor the public good which requires (modest) collective action. If Government were performing its proper functions, individuals and their families would have been launched into independence and increasing freedom and personal responsibility. They would be paying less to the State but would be spending more on their own provision for health and education. (Private health and education are socially responsible since the poor should not be contributing to the cost of such provision for those who can well afford their own.) Welfare and State subsidy should be directed at those who need it, not used as tax shelters and hidden perks by those perfectly able to provide for themselves. The main distinction between a society based on the emancipated individual and a society based on the controls and intervention of the State is the question of *openness*. Market capitalism and an emancipating State reveal the true nature of costs, prices, incomes, power and responsibility. The controlling State distorts costs through subsidy, disguises prices through manipulation, reduces incomes through high taxes (and then grants covert tax allowances to a favoured few) talks of "power to the people" but then reduces public choice and accuses its opponents of exploitation while protecting its own privileges at their expense. The controlling State underwrites the excesses of the foolish and then "rescues" them by enmeshing them in a web of "social" bureaucracy.

We have seen how the political notion of Democracy is based on occasional elections and dubious "opinion polls" asking questions for which there are only two possible answers – the ludicrous or the one the questioner wanted in the first place. We have seen how the political establishments (particularly on the Left) cannot tolerate an honest analysis of individual ill health since their collectivist power bases rely on political explanations of and collectivist excuses for individual irresponsiblity. Protest in the form of demonstrations, letter writing and political motions are not a sign of Democracy, they are proof that the individual citizen has little influence over his life and that his collective, political protests will merely give further justification to those institutions which are at the root of his discontent and democratic emasculation.

120

One of the man ironies of socialist collectivism is the failure of its most pernicious institution, the Trade Union Closed Shop, to do other than exploit those it claimed to be protecting – never mind the millions of non members who were effectively "taxed" by its activities.

The lessons of the closed shop can be applied to the entire principle of collective bargaining. The poorest workers *are* members of Trade Unions and the richest workers are *not*. Trade Unions can only gain short term advantage for the members who remain *after* their colleagues have been "sold" to pay for higher wages. In the long run even those who remain can only benefit if their industry is a protected monopoly or cartel which is a burden on the whole of society.

A critique of a State monopoly in the energy industry showed how price controls undermine the very definition of a business asset. Such controls led Government to act on the basis of a lie. The State committed to the import of resources which the country already possessed.

The increased power of the State and the ubiquitous tentacles of Government patronage soon turn economic analysts into their own servants. Where the State finances economic research it is easier for civil servants and academics to praise Government interventionist logic than to question it. Sycophantic economists, screened from ever suffering the consequences of their own conclusions, are as much a product of the corporatist and socialist State as are energy shortages, loss making industries and high taxes.

The 50 year economic history of the North South divide in the United Kingdom is one of the clearest examples of State failure. If ever the State failed to grasp even the rudiments of wealth creation and intervened to achieve the opposite of its intentions then the United Kingdom's interventionist "regional policy" is a prime example of this process. There are no better examples of how a natural organic process of decline, renewal and growth was turned, by Government, into a process of continual decline, economic waste and social alienation.

The appalling waste of the Mortgage Interest Tax Relief and its debilitating effects on the entire economy are all the more incomprehensible since the relief is sustained by a Conservative party which has rejected such interventionist logic in other areas.

The Democratic State was conceived as a fairer and more

efficient alternative to despotic monarchs, laissez faire capitalism and communist or fascist systems but is has acquired far greater and more arbitrary powers. We have seen how the inequalities between individuals of the same skills, education and social origins have grown as the power of the "democratic State" has increased. The reason for these injustices lies in the assumption that Democracy consists entirely of the universal franchise and the power of Government. Government's universal powers are far too attractive to be ignored by lobbyists and political and economic interest groups and those who control the levers of power are far too few and too remote to be accountable to the people in general.

An occasional electoral vote serves only to change the political horses. The unresponsive carriage of the State continues on its way. The alternative is a gradual but large reduction in the powers and aegis of the State as the emancipated people take on responsibility for themselves, their families, their businesses and their own social provision. The State will continue to support the needy, directly and not through the many middlemen of the "caring professions" whose ideas of social support often begin with their own salaries and end with the patronised and unemployable. There is a training budget within the Manpower Services Commission worth £3,000m per annum. Responsible for the distribution of this State largesse is a retired headmistress. Such a sum represents the equivalent of the capital of 300 substantial companies. Who is more likely to train, employ and enrich Britain's unskilled and unemployed a retired headmistress or the management teams of 300 large companies?

There are many important functions for the State – law and order, defence, welfare, road networks, fair trading and monopolies and mergers legislation. But these legitimate roles have been inadequately or incompetently pursued as Government saw far better avenues for political manipulation in fiscal subsidy, preferential legislation, the monopoly ownership of industry, the control of prices and the use of inflation both as a surreptitious tax and as a political disguise of privilege.

Those who are elected to hold public office can only hold the respect of the people in general if they concentrate on those tasks which individuals and free associations could *not* perform. Overstepping these boundaries in order to reward the politically acceptable turns Government into a form of sectarian feud with the democratic institutions attracting the wrath of at least half the population rather than the acceptance of all.

If these essays have induced even a modicum of doubt about the democratic credentials of Government the book will have achieved its purpose. But perhaps it may contribute to a general realisation that true Democracy is based principally on individual choice and responsibility rather than on an occasional vote and on the gradual withdrawal of the State rather than on its increasing social and economic intervention. The true despots seek out and preserve individual weakness as a source of their collectivist power. The true democratic servant is pleased to see his administrations become increasingly redundant.

OTHER BOOKS BY THE AUTHOR

THE EMANCIPATED SOCIETY

State Authority and Individual Freedom
ISBN 0 9509353 2 8 Hardback £10.95

The author rejects the traditional conflict between Right/ Capitalism and Left/Socialism and contrasts instead Emancipated and Dependent Societies. The former are based on individual freedom, competition, overt social signals and continuous "social challenge" to authority. The latter are based on collectivism, State control, covert agreements and subservience to authority. Left/Right "horizontal politics" is rejected in favour of the Authoritarian/Libertarian "vertical axis" of political choice. No one, says the author, not even Government "can be permitted to decide the terms according to which they will be deemed successful." The role of the State must be based on the consent of the subordinated, limited to those activities which **only** the State can perform and capable of reduction or expansion according to public choice.

Atkinson describes a direct link between increasing State control and collectivism and ever more violent forms of individual "deviation" from social norms. He contrasts Government taxation with competition – a more democratic and less distorting form of "tax", and describes legitimate (emancipating) and illegitimate (controlling) Government activities as well as criteria for Government withdrawal.

State power leads to **static** definitions of justice, wealth etc while the more directly democratic **public choice** can more justly accommodate **change**. The book provides a wealth of new concepts to characterise the relationship between the State and the individual: **the wrong consensus, just process, taxploitation, the dialectic of freedom, deviant energy, captive logic, circles of responsibility, social challenge** and the critical distinction between **emancipated** and **dependent** societies.

"A powerful argument that is economically literate, historically erudite and philosophically cogent. Its central distinction between emancipated and dependent societies ought to acquire a much more central role in political thought and discourse."   Dr. John Gray, Jesus College, Oxford.

"An illuminating beam of light and thought over the present confused landscape of political ideas."

          Rt. Hon. David Howell, MP.

"A brilliant polemic. Atkinson's celebration of the virtues of free exchange and spontaneous processes has shattered many collectivist illusions."

     Professor Norman Barry, University of Buckingham.

"An argument for the moral superiority of the free market taken further and deeper than I have heard it developed before. An analysis of a high order of clarity and rigour: a powerful contribution."   Crossbow.

The philosophical analysis of the "knowledge" on the basis of which universal Government decisions are applied, the **morality** of Government distortion of economic signals, the sociological explanation of individual "deviant energy" and the parallels drawn between linguistic and monetary signs make Atkinson's political economy an analysis of unusual intellectual breadth and depth.

GOVERNMENT
AGAINST THE PEOPLE

ISBN 0 9509353 1 X. Hardback £6.00

The book demonstrates the failure of the State and questions the very definition of Democratic Government. Part I describes the **political** process behind Government inspired inflation and describes the technical and moral case for monetarism.

Part II shows how Government industrial intervention and fiscal manipulation destroy more than they create – at the expense of those very groups Government claims to be helping. International examples of the failure of economic collectivism – the European Community, Trade controls and international debt – are analysed.

Part III shows how Governments, having wasted time in illegitimate intervention have then failed to provide the "public goods" which even market liberals agree are legitimate roles for the State. "The all powerful State soon earns the contempt of those it set out to protect and the friendship of those it set out to control."

"Excellent – a devastating catalogue of the depredations of Government against the people."

George Gilder, author Wealth and Poverty

"Excellent, fascinating."

Milton Friedman, Nobel Prize Winner in Economics

"An Excellent book." Matthew Parris, The Sunday Times

"Original and provocative insights ... excessive Government expertly diagnosed." Professor Norman Barry, University of Buckingham.